SUPERNATURAL
JOIN THE HUNT

THE OFFICIAL
COCKTAIL BOOK

SUPERNATURAL
JOIN THE HUNT

THE OFFICIAL COCKTAIL BOOK

By Adam Carbonell and James Asmus

INSIGHT EDITIONS

SAN RAFAEL • LOS ANGELES • LONDON

holy Water

CONTENTS

THE ROAD SO FAR . . .

Ghosts. Monsters. Demons.

If you read those words and expect imaginary tales of equally unreal dangers, you may have grabbed the wrong book. However, if you've faced one of these horrors—or are prepared to accept the reality of them—we are happy to be your guide.

By accepting the truth of what's out there, and not running in fear for some safe place to forget, you're on the path of the hunters—people who stick their necks out into the darkness, no matter what might be waiting to bite. Some hunters take up arms to chase evil and action anywhere they may find it, while other hunters pore through books and keep a fortified homestead. Whatever kind you aim to be, the knowledge in these pages will up your game—and just might save your life.

Of course, much of the secrets contained here wouldn't be known if not for two hunters in particular, Sam and Dean Winchester. While countless hunters have laid down their lives to save others, these brothers laid down theirs *several* times. And just as often, they saved the entire world. But their work was in the shadows, so too few know of their exceptional run.

This book was compiled, in part, as a tribute, its pages a cocktail of its own sort, offering glimpses into the lives of the Winchester brothers. Its recipes are mixed with the secrets and insights uncovered in their years of fighting every unholy threat from Hell and Earth (plus some holy ones). But as their cases, trials, and tribulations could fill countless books (and, in fact, have, documented by Carver Edlund), in this volume, that tribute is paid by focusing on one of the brothers' true passions: drinking.

A good drink (alcoholic or not) can offer a hunter focus, comfort, reward, even intel on those around them. It's no surprise that when new hunters are looking to learn more about the legends who came before them or the threats that lie ahead, plenty of answers and anecdotes are reflected in a cocktail glass.

For the first time, the bar orders and observations of heroes, gods, and monsters are collected here, compiled from the Winchesters' own notes and personal accounts of other folks who crossed their paths or called them friends. Sam and Dean have earned their peace. But their fight deserves to be remembered, learned from, and passed down like lore.

So, pour some salt, raise a glass, and carry on—into the SUPERNATURAL.

A KILLER ARSENAL

Same as you wouldn't head out on a hunt without stocking up your weapons first, you'd best check whether you've got all the essential tools before you stick your neck out into the recipes ahead. Sure, you might be able to save the day with whatever you have on hand—but if you plan to kill a werewolf, you buy some silver bullets, right? Well, if you plan to stalk your way through these pages, the following will be your silver bullets, crosses, and iron. (And hell, maybe get a second set to keep in the trunk of your baby, just in case.)

GLASSWARE

Ultimately, what matters is what's in the glass, not the glass itself. But if you want to elevate your cocktail game and overall enjoyment, the vessel in which you present that cocktail is important. For sours, Manhattans, and martinis, a 4-to-6-ounce stemmed coupe glass is a perfect multiuse investment. Otherwise, a classic Nick and Nora or a traditional martini glass would be a fine substitute. A 20-ounce hurricane glass for blended or crushed-ice cocktails is another solid choice, and of course, no home bar is complete without a workhorse set of rocks and highball glasses. The julep cup, double old-fashioned, tumbler, collins, margarita, and clear Irish coffee mug are some other nice additions, if you have the space.

For beer, a classic 16-ounce pint and a stemmed tulip, or Belgian, glass will suffice.

Last is the never-ending money pit that is tiki mug collecting. You name it, there's a tiki mug design for it—a devilish and rewarding hobby, to say the least.

BAR SPOONS

Not only is the bar spoon the workhorse of stirred cocktails, but this versatile tool can also be used to diffuse liquids for layering, can split large cubes of ice, and is considered a unit of measurement when building your cocktails (it translates to half a teaspoon). A good 15-inch (40-centimeter) bar spoon with a tight spiral coil is recommended, but there are extra-long variations. Some have useful end tools, such as muddlers. Other additions may be fairly useless but super cool-looking, like the ornamental trident tailpiece.

SHAKERS

The two most commonly used shakers are the two-piece Boston and the three-piece cobbler shaker. The iconic cobbler, with its sleek and sexy design, is actually a major pain to use. The lids are prone to getting stuck, and the design isn't very versatile. A Boston shaker set is the best choice for all your cocktail shaking needs, specifically, a set of weighted shaking tins, as opposed to the less-efficient glass pint that may chip or break.

ICE

Ice matters. A lot. Invest in a good set of ice molds, unless you want to shell out hundreds, if not thousands, on a proper ice machine, and always use good water. Distilled or properly filtered is best. Again, ice is an ingredient, so take it as seriously as your choice in spirit. There are many great molds for large cubes or spheres, but once you've achieved ice-making perfection, you'll need to store it properly. You don't want your ice, and subsequently your cocktail, to taste like last week's frozen dinner, so store your well-made ice away from the odors and funk that could be hanging around your freezer.

JIGGER

If you want to achieve precision and consistency when making cocktails, you'll need to measure your ingredients. For this, we use a jigger—sometimes two. Most cocktails are measured in ounces. A good double-sided jigger is best for speed, efficiency, and precision and can accurately measure a range from ½ ounce to 2 ounces. Whichever you choose, a measured approach is the right approach.

MUDDLER

Some ingredients need a little forcing. For that, we muddle. When trying to incorporate fresh fruit, herbs, and spices into a cocktail, a good, sturdy muddler is the tool of choice. Whether wood, stainless steel, or food-grade plastic, find one with a flat bottom, as opposed to a textured tip, which can get a little aggressive. Save your aggression for the ghouls.

STRAINERS

Another vital tool for every level of bartending is the humble strainer. Specifically, the Hawthorne strainer. This is the most common and versatile cocktail strainer on the market. Good for separating the cocktail from ice and removing large particles such as fruit and pulp, specifically used when shaking drinks. Most professionals use a Hawthorne in tandem with a coned fine mesh strainer. This ensures no small particulates of pulp or ice make their way into the finished cocktail. Finally, there's the julep strainer. Perfect for spirit-forward stirred cocktails where small particulates are not a concern. A Hawthorne also works perfectly fine here.

PEELER

A sturdy Y-peeler will suffice for most, if not all, your peeling needs. Just be sure to master the technique. The Y-peeler is *the* cause of many a bartender's early shift exit to the emergency room as a result of accidentally removing a piece of themselves. Hold the fruit with your palm angled toward your face, creating a peeler-sized gap between your thumb and forefinger. Gently peel toward yourself, top to bottom, for citrus-garnish perfection.

CITRUS PRESSES AND JUICERS

Spend the money and get yourself a good-quality hand juicer or press. Go big but not too big. A lemon juicer will suffice for most cocktail-juicing needs. For larger fruit, cut down to size. If you're looking to expand into juices beyond the humble lemon, orange, and lime, invest in a good mechanical juicer.

DROPPERS

Great for controlled drops of bitters on top of a beautifully made whiskey sour, or for proofing down a nice glass of whiskey with cold water.

STORAGE

Cheap and reusable deli containers (8-, 16-, and 32-ounces) are a solid investment for storing batched drinks, infused spirits, garnishes, or any cocktail experiment needs. Flip top glass, or stainless, airtight containers are also ideal for a more sustainable—though much pricier—storage solution. Also consider a few deli style squeeze, or glass dash, bottles for easy distribution of syrups and tinctures.

CUTTING BOARD

For all your garnish-cutting needs, choose a small 8-to-10-inch food-grade plastic or wooden cutting board that can be stowed easily. If using wood, be sure to treat it with a cutting board wood oil.

KITCHEN SCALE

Some ingredients are better measured in weight. For this, a small, reliable kitchen scale will suffice. A digital scale with a variety of measurement options from grams to pounds is very versatile and also great for baking and cooking.

CHEESECLOTH

For when you need more straining power than a sieve or fine meshed strainer can offer. This is essential for fat-washing. A coffee filter makes for a suitable substitute.

KNIFE

A simple, inexpensive paring knife for cutting garnish and other ingredients. Serrated is a solid option for those who don't sharpen their own knives. Just make sure to keep the kitchen kind separate from any hunting knives. Rugaru juice will likely spoil even the best mixed cocktail.

LEWIS BAG AND MALLET

Simply put, a canvas sack and a whacking stick. A fantastic stress reliever for controlled ice-crushing goodness. With a good Lewis bag and mallet, you can crack, crush, or obliterate your ice according to each cocktail's needs.

WINE OPENERS AND BOTTLE OPENERS

Get yourself a good pocket-size, double-hinged wine key or multi-tool. Most have a small knife for cutting off the foil and contain a simple bottle opener. When talking bar tools, simple is always best.

MIXING GLASSES

Other than material, typically glass or stainless steel, the main variation in mixing glasses is decorative. Used primarily for spirit-forward cocktails, such as Manhattans and martinis, where dilution and aeration are minimal, and chilling can be controlled with precision.

FUNNEL

A simple funnel, with a spout that fits inside the mouth of a bottle, is perfect for bottling infused spirits or when batching cocktails.

COCKTAIL PICKS

Cocktail picks are perfect for skewering decorative garnishes and elevating the visual game of any home bartender. There are many options, from a simple disposable bamboo pick to a reusable stainless-steel skewer, or you can even get creative with a sprig of rosemary.

ICE TOOLS

Ice picks, tongs, and buckets are all very useful—but not necessary—tools of the trade. If you have the space, spruce it up with a few functional ice tools. If you can afford to spring for pure silver, most can double as weapons against werewolves and skinwalkers!

ZESTERS AND MICROPLANES

You can use a box cheese grater in a pinch, but one good handheld zester is the perfect tool for efficient cocktail garnishing, whether grating nutmeg or zesting fresh citrus in or atop a cocktail.

SPRITZ AND SPRAY BOTTLES

A few 2-to-4-ounce spray bottles are great for misting your glassware or cocktail with spirits or other ingredients for an elevated experience. A couple sprays of absinthe on a Sazerac or some peated scotch on top of a Penicillin adds the perfect amount, and the act is a much more appealing visual than a quick rinse and dump.

RIMMING GLASSWARE

Sometimes the secret ingredient is on the outside of the cocktail. Whether salt, sugar, or spice, a well-rimmed cocktail can enhance your drink and add a visual pop in the process. For citrus-forward cocktails, simply rub a slice of lemon, lime, or orange around the rim of your chosen glassware and dip, spin, or roll in your desired salt, sugar, or spice mixture. For a bolder approach, use simple or flavored syrups on your glassware as an adhesive substitute, such as the bold and spicy chamoy to adhere your spice mix on a Bloody Mary or Michelada.

AROMATIC BITTERS

From medicinal snake oil to indispensable ingredient of bartenders the world over, bitters are a key weapon in any home bartender's arsenal. In many ways, bitters are the spice of the cocktail kingdom. Not only do bitters balance and enhance many classic cocktails, they also add an aromatic component. The original heavy hitters like Angostura, orange, and Peychaud's lend a wonderful herbal bitterness and aroma while newer offerings come in an endless variety of flavor concepts. Grapefruit, chocolate, rhubarb, and creole are just a few examples of today's bitters innovations.

PRESERVED CHERRIES

Whether pickled or fortified with alcohol, the cherry is the staple garnish to many a cocktail. Most famous is the sweetened maraschino. Just try to avoid the bleached and dyed imposters found at many favorite dives and neighborhood haunts. There are plenty of great brands out there, like Luxardo, but they do get pricey. Luckily, whether maraschino or brandied, there are plenty of great, simple recipes available for making your own at home. Here's an easy, no-cook recipe for a fortified cherry made at home using bourbon.

BOURBON MARASCHINO CHERRIES

1 pound whole (pitted) cherries

¼ cup Rich Demerara Sugar Syrup (page 13)

5 ounces bourbon

3 ounces Luxardo maraschino liqueur

1 teaspoon vanilla extract

In a 32-ounce deli container or canning jar, place your pitted cherries and top with Rich Demerara Sugar Syrup, vanilla extract, Luxardo liqueur, and bourbon. With the lid on, give everything a good shake and set aside to age—2 weeks in a cool, dark corner of the kitchen is recommended. Refrigerate for longer shelf life and enjoy!

EGGS AND EGG ALTERNATIVES

DON'T FEAR THE EGG! Embrace it! Whether using just the white or the whole egg, eggs are a great way to enhance the texture, mouthfeel, and volume of a cocktail. Eggs are your friends and, more importantly, your cocktail's. If you are a little skittish about cracking fresh eggs into a cocktail, there are plenty of pasteurized packaged alternatives. If you have a dietary restriction or want a vegan alternative, don't fret. Aquafaba is a fantastic substitution. Simply put, aquafaba is the viscous water solution found within a can of chickpeas. Use 2 to 3 tablespoons of aquafaba in lieu of the white from 1 egg.

DEHYDRATD FRUITS

A dehydrated citrus wheel makes for a nice visual impact atop or clipped to the side of a cocktail. If you have a dehydrator, great, but it's not necessary. For a perfectly dehydrated citrus wheel—or other fruit of your choice—simply slice the fruit into ¼-inch rounds and place on a baking sheet, or wire rack, in the oven at 170° to 200°F (76° to 93°C) for 3 to 6 hours. A lime will take much less time than a grapefruit.

SUGARS, SYRUPS, AND SWEETENERS

Most balanced cocktail recipes call for some sort of sweetener. You can use muddled sugar, but most professionals choose a sweetened syrup, which will integrate better into the cocktail (see Holy Waters). The "sweet" can also come in the form of a sweetened spirit, such as the vermouth in a manhattan. A one-to-one ratio of heated water to sugar is typical. This is also a great opportunity to add flavors to sweetened syrups. Cinnamon, ginger, and vanilla are great versatile options. If there's one area where you can experiment on a budget, this is it. For the sweet, play with a variety of sugars, honeys, and syrups. For added flavor, try spices, fruits, and herbs. Just make sure to strain your syrup clean before storing away for future cocktail endeavors.

CHAMOY

A sweet, sour, and spicy Mexican syrup made from pickled fruits and chilis. Great for rimming glassware and as an ingredient for a spicy-sour kick.

HOLY WATERS

A hunter is always prepared with a few prebottled lifesavers at the ready: holy water, holy oil, Dead Man's Blood . . . . As a mixologist, you'd be just as smart to keep a few of the following "go-to" magic potions on hand. These simple syrups are used as building blocks in several recipes you'll find in this book. Plus, once you learn how to use them, who knows all the ways they could come to the rescue?

SIMPLE SYRUP

1 cup granulated sugar

1 cup water

This basic simple syrup recipe is the workhorse of many a craft cocktail and is super easy to make and store at home. Bring water to a boil and remove from heat. Add sugar and stir until dissolved. Let cool, then transfer syrup to a sealed bottle or container. Keep refrigerated for up to a month.

RICH DEMERARA SYRUP

2 cups demerara or turbinado sugar

1 cup water

Rich syrups are great for heartier whiskey and rum cocktails, or anywhere you want to add a rich sweetness without the dilution. Bring water to a boil and remove from heat. Add sugar and stir until dissolved. Let cool, then transfer syrup to a sealed bottle or container. Keep refrigerated for up to a month.

CINNAMON VANILLA SYRUP

2 cups demerara or turbinado sugar (can substitute with honey)

1 cup water

3 cinnamon sticks

1 split vanilla bean (optional)

This rich syrup infusion adds the slight savory boost of cinnamon, but you can sub out the cinnamon with a variety of other flavorful spices such as allspice, clove, or cardamon to name a few, using the same technique. Bring water, vanilla, and cinnamon to a boil and remove from heat. Add sugar and stir until dissolved. Let cool, then transfer syrup to a sealed bottle or container. Keep refrigerated for up to a month.

BUTTERFLY PEA SYRUP

½ cup butterfly pea flowers

1 cup water

1 cup granulated white sugar

A simple syrup infusion that when introduced to a little acid turns deep purple for a fantastic visual effect. Heat water to a simmer and remove from heat. Add flowers and let steep for 5 minutes. Strain into a container and stir in sugar until combined. Can be stored in an airtight container in the refrigerator for several weeks.

SHRUB

1 pint ripe strawberries

1 cup demerara or turbinado sugar

½ cup vinegar (apple, malt, or red wine work well for berries)

An ancient preservation technique that adds a delightful fresh, fruity, and tart flavor to your home cocktails or can be diluted with seltzer for a refreshing non-alcoholic treat. Trim off the strawberry tops and cut the berries in half. In a bowl, add sugar to strawberries and let macerate for up to 2 days in the refrigerator. Meanwhile, add the discarded tops to the vinegar to reduce waste and fortify the vinegar with a little more flavor. Strain the strawberry flesh from the finished syrup and from the vinegar and combine the syrup with vinegar to create your shrub.

GINGER HONEY SYRUP

1 cup honey (or agave nectar for a vegan-friendly substitution)

1 cup water

¾ cup sliced ginger

A uniquely sweet and savory ingredient that has excellent cocktail applications and is also great in teas and desserts. Heat the honey, water, and ginger in a saucepan and bring to a boil. Reduce to a low simmer for 3 minutes. Remove from heat and let steep for 30 minutes. Let cool and strain into an airtight container. Can be stored in the refrigerator for several weeks.

GRENADINE SYRUP

2 cups pomegranate juice

2 cups sugar

2 ounces pomegranate molasses

1 teaspoon orange blossom water (or orange bitters)

Here's a natural and simple alternative to the recognizable day-glo red bottles of grenadine found in the supermarket, which are chock-full of nasty ingredients and preservatives. In a small saucepan, heat pomegranate juice to a simmer and add sugar. Turn off heat and stir until dissolved. Stir in pomegranate molasses and orange blossom water. Transfer to a sealed container or bottle and keep in refrigerator.

ORGEAT SYRUP

3 cups white sugar

2 cups unsweetened almond milk

1 teaspoon orange blossom water

½ teaspoon rose water

½ teaspoon almond extract

This nutty and citrusy syrup is the secret weapon of many a tiki drink with a wide range of other cocktail applications. In a medium saucepan, combine sugar and almond milk. Stir over medium-low heat until sugar is completely dissolved. Remove from heat and add orange blossom water, rose water, and almond extract. Stir to combine and transfer to a sealed container or bottle and keep in refrigerator.

BACON-WASHED BOURBON

16 ounces smoked thick-cut bacon (the smokier, the better)

One 750-milliliter bottle bourbon

Cook your bacon on the stove, or in the oven on a sheet pan. Once bacon is cooked to desired doneness and the fat is rendered, set aside for a spicy maple glazing (page 127). Pour rendered fat into a nonreactive container and mix with bourbon. Use a whisk or immersion blender to combine. Transfer the bourbon (save the bottle for later) and fat mixture to the freezer for at least 2 hours. At this point, the fat will have risen to the top and solidified. Simply remove the layer of fat, or poke a large hole and, using a strainer, some cheesecloth, or a coffee filter and a funnel, filter the washed bourbon back into the empty bourbon bottle and store in the refrigerator.

FAMILY RECIPES

There's no way to summarize all the forces, family, and experiences that shaped Sam and Dean Winchester. But as boys who lost both parents to demons, were raised on the road in the hunt, and spent their lives getting dragged between Heaven and Hell (and all the horrors between), they sure deserved a drink. While they more than earned it with every life saved or monster slain, the truth is, the boys were known to turn to each other instead for their strength, solace, and relief. Though we may not know the private conversations that kept them going, plenty heard the love and bond they shared every time one talked about the other or the mom and dad they'd lost.

On the other hand, if you got them talking over a couple of drinks, whether waxing nostalgic or telling embarrassing tales about each other, you'd catch bits of Sam and Dean's personal ups and downs shining through. The recipes here are ones their friends might feel reveal some essence or moment of their lives. And generally, like the boys themselves, these are a little more no-nonsense but can still pack a punch.

56

SAM'S DÄMONENJÄGER

In the beginning, Sam Winchester was a bright and promising prelaw student at Stanford—before his big brother Dean and all the forces of Heaven and Hell came storming back to him with other plans. But in that brief time of independence, Sammy embraced a "normal" life with a spirit somewhere between escape and rebellion. Here his college drink of choice, Jägermeister, mixes into a cocktail just as conflicted and complex. Honey sweetens the dark influence of Jäger, while ginger and lime offer distraction and break the liquor out into new territory. Adding soda water dilutes the internal clashes just enough to make it all settle down easier.

1½ ounces Jägermeister
¾ ounce Ginger Honey Syrup (page 14)
½ ounce fresh lime juice
4 ounces seltzer
1 lime wheel, for garnish

Shake Jägermeister, Ginger Honey Syrup, and lime juice with ice. Strain into an ice-filled highball glass, add soda, and give it one or two good stirs. Garnish with a lime wheel.

STILL KICKING

Dean Winchester is a simple man with simple tastes. Classic cars. Cold beers. Strong whiskey. Dead monsters. But if he's got a full bar and some time to kill or a story to tell, he's likely to splash in just a little complexity to keep things interesting. In this case, spicy rye mixes with sharp but refreshing ginger beer to give a lively kick (and feel the kick of still being alive), while the bitters stop things from getting too saccharine and deepen this drink's brooding appeal.

---

2 ounces rye

2 dashes Peychaud's Bitters

4 to 5 ounces ginger beer

1 lemon twist, for garnish

Add ingredients to an ice-filled collins or highball, stir, and garnish with a lemon twist.

WAYWARD SONS

Even the simplest combinations can be unforgettably potent. When Sam and Dean Winchester came together, for example, their bond gave them strength, balance, and saved the world more than once. This simple cocktail blends their signature spirits, bringing balance and opening up in ways they never would without the other. The result is just as unique and compelling as chronicles of the boys themselves—with plenty of dark smoke, some bitterness, some sweetness, and just enough brightness to carry you home.

1½ ounces Jägermeister
1½ ounces rye
2 dashes orange bitters
1 dehydrated citrus wheel, for garnish

Stir together Jägermeister and rye in an ice-filled rocks glass. Top with bitters and garnish with a dehydrated citrus wheel.

PURPLE NURPLE

When a grad student (who may or may not have been named Starla) first introduced Dean to "Purple Nurples" in a barroom investigation, the hunter was pleasantly surprised by these sweet, fruity shots. Just as each of the brothers has his own version of how that case went down, this is a unique version of the drink. This take is a bit classier (just like . . . "not Starla," who studied anthropology and folklore), using some bittersweet and sour elements to balance the fruit taste, while keeping it bright and frisky.

---

2 ounces Clement coconut liqueur
½ ounce curaçao
½ ounce crème de mûre
¾ ounce fresh lime juice
1 lime wheel, or 2 blackberries on a skewer, for garnish

Shake all ingredients and double-strain into a coupe or martini glass. Garnish with a lime wheel or blackberries using a cocktail pick. Can also be split between two shot glasses and served as shooters.

CHRISTMAS SPIRITS EGGNOG

A hunter's life tends to blur into one big mess of monsters, miles, and motels. And that makes the big days on the calendar all the more important. Whether it's a holiday or an anniversary of something good, bad, or near-apocalyptic, pausing to mark a meaningful date offers a break from the grind. These occasions often remind us where we've been, the time we've had, and who or what keeps us going.

When Sam and Dean had the chance to stop and breathe long enough to mark a Christmas together, it was to share simple gifts and family memories over cups of eggnog. While festive liquor can be spiked into any store-bought nog, this homemade mix offers a full flavor that truly comes together for a special toast.

1½ ounces bonded bourbon

½ ounce rum, preferably a rum agricole

¾ ounce Cinnamon Vanilla Syrup (page 14)

1 ounce heavy cream

1 whole egg

Cinnamon and nutmeg, for garnish

Dry-shake all ingredients, add ice, and shake again until chilled. Double-strain into a chilled old-fashioned glass. Garnish with a combination of finely grated nutmeg and cinnamon.

YELLOW-EYED COOLER

Tales of the Winchester brothers aren't just revered and retold among hunters in the know. The boys unwittingly became the subjects of a series of novels, written by Carver Edlund (a pen name for Chuck Shurley). While the books were thought to be prophecies—until revealed to be the Word of God, himself—to the world at large, they were simply works of fiction with a modest but passionate fan base.

As with any devoted fandom, there was eventually a fan convention to discuss and celebrate the books and everything related. While this particular cocktail for the event, the Yellow-Eyed Cooler, may have been named in questionable taste (after the demon that killed Sam and Dean's mother), its actual taste will please those looking for a zesty, cool, and fruity drink to go with the latest page-turner.

1½ ounces white rum
¾ ounce fresh lemon juice
½ ounce pineapple
¾ ounce Simple Syrup (page 13)
4 to 5 ounces pilsner beer
2 fresh pineapple balls

Shake rum, lemon juice, pineapple, and Simple Syrup and double-strain into a hurricane glass. Top with pilsner and give a stir. Garnish with 2 melon-balled pineapple eyes on a garnish pick.

MARY'S REWARD

Whatever instinct Sam and Dean have for "taking care of business," they must have inherited from their mother. Mary Winchester (née Campbell) was a sharp and extremely capable hunter, cutting her way through the evil things of the world since childhood. When her love, John Winchester, died, she struck a deal to bring him back. From then on, she took care of her husband, their sons, and the things going bump in the night. If there was one thing Mary neglected to take care of, it was herself.

If you find yourself like Mary, burning the candle (or the ghost's tether) at both ends, this mix offers some quick and easy "self-care" (not that she'd call it that). Mary never was one to cook, but mixing a hearty dose of fresh fruit into some relaxing and refreshing white wine is an easy way to knock out a couple of needs at once. And you've got to take care of yourself before you can take care of a family—or the next monster.

---

1 750-milliliter bottle dry white wine

3 cups sliced fruit, such as peach, grapes, mango, orange, or whatever is fresh and not too dark in color—the fresher, the better

¼ cup St-Germain Liqueur

¼ cup pear brandy

¼ cup Luxardo maraschino liqueur

2 to 3 mint sprigs, for garnish

2 to 3 fresh orange slices, for garnish

2 to 3 fresh berries, for garnish

Add all ingredients into a pitcher or punch bowl and refrigerate up to one day in advance. Serve in a wineglass with ice. Garnish with mint sprigs (make sure to give the mint a light slap to express its fragrant oils) and a few slices of fresh orange and berries of your choice.

DAD'S OLD-FASHIONED

John Winchester was an almost bygone kind of American man. Bootstrapped himself up at an early age, after his father disappeared. Served in the Marine Corps in Vietnam. Started a mechanic business after, back in Kansas. Fell in love. Became a doggedly protective father. But ultimately let his work keep him from his family more than they wished. The thing is, later in life, John's work was as a hunter.

Just like Sam and Dean's dad, this drink is equal parts sweet and sour. And its apple brandy and old-fashioned-style mix is just as vintage American. But maybe it's most fitting to say that both are undeniably strong in spirit.

---

2 ounces Laird's apple brandy

½ ounce Rich Demerara Sugar Syrup (page 13)

2 to 3 dashes grapefruit bitters

1 fresh grapefruit peel, for garnish

Build the cocktail in an ice-filled double old-fashioned glass and stir until combined. If possible, use one large, molded ice cube or sphere. Garnish with grapefruit peel—be sure to express the oils over the cocktail by rubbing the peel around the rim before placing atop the cocktail.

The grapefruit bitters brings out the fruitiness of the spirit. Flavorful and balanced, there's nothing weak about this one.

ANOTHER BROTHER SHANDY

There was only a short time where Adam Milligan knew he had two half-brothers, and shorter still the time Sam and Dean had to spend with their father's youngest son. Adam enjoyed a normal life, unaware of the types of monsters that had brought John Winchester briefly into his mother's life or the demons he'd tragically face in the end. Simply being of Winchester blood meant getting dragged into the conflicts between Heaven and Hell, life and death, and the Winchesters against the Apocalypse. In the end, Adam sacrificed himself to save humanity. So, cheers to an oft-overlooked Winchester, who died (more than once) for our sins. In his honor, this half-and-half shandy gives its sweet starters a sharp and more bitter end.

1⅓ ounces nonpeated scotch
¾ ounce lemon juice
½ ounce Simple Syrup (page 13)
1 ounce grapefruit liqueur
3 to 4 ounces hazy IPA
1 dehydrated grapefruit wheel

Shake scotch, lemon juice, Simple Syrup, and grapefruit liqueur (like Giffard Crème de Pamplemousse) and double-strain into a beer tulip or large wineglass. Add the IPA. Garnish with a dehydrated grapefruit wheel.

VELVET

BABY'S OWN

No account of the Winchester family would be complete without special tribute to the loved one most reliably and consistently in their lives—their jet-black 1967 Impala. "Baby," as Dean so lovingly calls her, was handed down to the boys from their father. And between spending most of their childhood riding around the country as John Winchester hunted, then putting a few hundred-thousand miles into pursuing their own destinies, Baby carried the boys from cradle to the grave (a few times) as a constant companion and the closest thing they ever had to a home. Fittingly, this concoction delivers comforting and homey flavor notes, including clove, nutmeg, and allspice, in an especially smooth, dark-bodied experience.

---

2 ounces Guinness Draught (Nitro)
1 ounce dark rum
½ ounce falernum
1 whole egg
Chocolate bitters
Freshly grated nutmeg, for garnish

Dry-shake Guinness, rum, falernum, and egg. Shake again with ice until chilled, and double-strain into coupe or fizzio. Using a dropper, garnish the top with a few drops of chocolate bitters and some fine-ground nutmeg.

FRIENDS OF THE FAMILY

When the things you go hunting for are likely hunting you, too, you want a good friend to watch your back. Of course, going toe-to-toe with unnatural evil and things from beyond the grave isn't for everybody. The work attracts a wide array of characters just about as colorful as the monsters. There are plenty of wingnuts, DOA rookies, and damaged loners it's best you stay away from. But at least for Sam and Dean Winchester, these are the friends and folks who were most meaningful (or most persistent) when the boys were fighting down in the trenches of their holy war. Like the people who inspired them, the drinks in this section have a broad range of style, origin, and strength. And now you've got them on call for whatever occasion you need them.

IDJIT RELIEF

Bobby Singer was a legendary hunter, well after what most men would call their prime. Even after losing the use of his legs, Bobby helped other hunters with leads, research into lore, and pretending to be an FBI supervisor (or any other necessary alibi) when friends in the field needed him. But to Sam and Dean Winchester, he embodied the notion that "family don't end with blood." Bobby came to be the uncle they never had and the father figure they often needed. (To let them know when they were being "idjits.") Of course, a rough life of worrying about folks, taking more than your share of scrapes, and having to yell sense into knuckleheads calls for backwoods medicine, like this particular prescription for some homemade tea with a healthy dose of cheap whiskey or bourbon. While he might never have gussied up his rotgut with a "clove-studded citrus wheel," Bobby sure would've done it for others if they needed him to.

---

2 ounces bonded bourbon (like White Dog)

1 ounce Ginger Honey Syrup (page 14)

4 ounces hot water

½ ounce lemon juice

1 clove-studded citrus wheel

Add bourbon, Ginger Honey Syrup, and lemon juice to an Irish coffee mug and stir in the hot water. Garnish with a cinnamon stick and a clove-studded citrus wheel. To create the wheel, use the tip of a paring knife to make a small slit around the outer lemon rind. Insert the cloves about ½ to 1 inch apart in the slit all around the wheel.

THE HARVELLE

Grab a double glass in remembrance of two fine hunters and finer hearts, Ellen and Jo Harvelle. This mother-daughter duo offered a homestead and surrogate family to others in lonesome monster-slaying life. After her husband Bill died on a hunt with John Winchester, Ellen ran Harvelle's Roadhouse as a safe haven, base of operations, and the rare spot for hunters to talk openly about the harrowing horrors they've survived. The rare comfort of a genuinely understanding ear was only improved by home cooking and healthily poured alcohol. And both were beloved, well before they sacrificed themselves to destroy Lucifer's Hellhounds.

This particular Roadhouse favorite is just as strong, subtly sweet, and welcoming as the Harvelles. Irish whiskey offers a smooth landing, and the chocolate and citrus notes remind us of the sweeter things in life. But the grounded, earthy nature of Cynar adds a bittersweet air.

---

2 ounces Irish whiskey

1 ounce Cynar

3 dashes orange bitters

1 orange peel, for garnish

Combine ingredients into a double old-fashioned glass with a large ice cube or sphere. Stir until combined and chilled. Garnish with an orange peel.

MORE THAN BLOOD

There aren't many hunters who manage to live a long life, given the work. But Sheriff Jody Mills has always been a cut above. You can imagine the extra work it took to prove her mettle and earn her rank at a relatively early age in North Dakota law enforcement. But nothing prepared Jody for the grim discovery that monsters were real—and her own lost son returned as a zombie. The horror and heartbreak she experienced would destroy most people. Instead, Jody added monsters, ghosts, and demons to her long list of responsibilities.

Within a few years, Sheriff Mills had taken on a couple other things, too—an impressive track record for putting down vampires (among other creeps), and a surrogate family of women whose lives were wrecked by their encounters with monsters. Jody embodied the idea that family is "more than blood." So, the bloodred color is a striking and tongue-in-cheek tribute on its own. But the veins of bitter Campari and lemon are punctured with every bite of grape, and the champagne connects the disparate flavors in a light and delightful home.

---

5 to 7 grapes
1 ounce gin
1 ounce Campari
¾ ounce lemon
½ ounce Simple Syrup (page 13)
1½ ounces champagne
1½ ounces soda water
2 grapes, for garnish
1 orange peel, for garnish

Muddle grapes in your shaking tin, then add gin, Campari, lemon, and Simple Syrup. Shake with ice before straining into an ice-filled wineglass. Top with soda water and champagne and give a couple stirs. Top with a skewered garnish of orange peel and grapes.

STUDY BUDDY

Since the earliest eras of mankind, God chose a prophet to receive and spread his word on Earth. Unfortunately for Kevin Tran, when his number came up to serve this purpose, it upended years of working toward a fancy college and dreams of a more lucrative, less apocalyptic future. But those marathon study sessions prepared Kevin for his destiny—to translate ancient tablets transcribed in heavenly tongue and uncover secrets to killing Leviathans, locking Hell, and so much more. Still, a 72-hour cram session to save the world (or at least the Winchesters' necks) doesn't leave much time for anything else. Enter: this cocktail! No one knows whether the recipe was handed down from on high or was the hallucination of an exhausted mind. Yet the light protein of egg white and bits of zesty nutrition from real lemon and apple help keep the doctor—and hopefully, demonic danger du jour—away. Its overall taste blends the almond flavor of orgeat and floral sweetness of St-Germain to at least *feel* as if you're enjoying a natural, balanced life.

1½ ounces calvados
¾ ounce St-Germain Liqueur
¾ ounce lemon juice
¼ ounce orgeat
1 egg white
Apple, for garnish
Angostura bitters

Dry-shake the calvados, St-Germain, lemon, orgeat, and egg white. Add ice and shake again. Double-strain into a coupe. For garnish, cut one side of an apple into thin slices. Fan the apple slices upward and skewer with a pick. A few decorative drops of Angostura bitters, and the cocktail is complete.

MRS. TRAN'S PINA COLADA

Just in case you ever find your life reduced to years of hiding out in an endless series of safe houses and mystically warded shacks in the middle of nowhere, keep this recipe handy. Consider Linda Tran. After all the ways she supported, pushed, and inspired her son Kevin to do his best and prepare for a bright future, his destiny was a million miles from what she'd dreamed of. And when her relationship to the conduit of cosmically important and dangerous knowledge made her the target of a power-hungry Crowley, it meant no more vacations (or going outside in general) for Mrs. Tran. But the lively tang of pineapple shining out between creamy, sweet, and soothing coconut and rum can make even the longest lockdown feel like a tropical escape.

---

2 ounces white rum
½ ounce blackstrap rum
1½ ounces pineapple juice
1½ ounces coconut cream
1 cup (4 ounces) pineapple chunks
2 cups ice
1 pineapple wedge, for garnish
2 pineapple leaves, for garnish

Add all the ingredients into a blender and blend until incorporated and smooth, about 10 seconds on high. Serve in a hurricane glass. Garnish with a slice of fresh pineapple and a couple of leaves pulled from the top of the fruit.

EMERALD BADASS

Computer coding. Hacking. LARPing. Witch slaying. Is there anything Charlie Bradbury couldn't do? For as much as she helped Sam and Dean from behind the keyboard or IRL, Charlie became a level-20 legend in the Land of Oz. After teaming up with the real-life Dorothy to defeat the Wicked Witch in our world, the two returned to the magical realm to free all the lions and tigers and bears from evil still reigning.

This emerald homage to her epic achievements gets its green from absinthe, with all its distinct anise flavor. The mint liqueur and orange curaçao add a sweetness and surprising layers to the star's natural sharpness. Just be careful how many you order at the next comic-con.

---

2 ounces absinthe
½ ounce lime juice
½ ounce crème de menthe
2 ounces soda water
2 lime wheels, for garnish
2 mint sprigs, for garnish

Shake absinthe, lime and crème de menthe. Strain into an ice-filled highball glass and top with soda water. For garnish place two lime wheels in the glass and top with a couple sprigs of mint.

CHEERFUL BOOTLEGGER

Look here, it doesn't get much more Minnesota than a Bootlegger cocktail or Donna Hanscum! One is the state's lone, lasting contribution to the world of mixing drinks, and the other is a lone law-woman turned lasting ally, mixing it up with the world of monsters! Donna may have been blindsided once (okay, or twice) by all this cuckoo supernatural stuff in her days as sheriff. But once those Winchester boys and Jody Mills opened her eyes, by golly, she was determined to keep good folks safe from that stuff, too! So, what's a pleased-as-punch daughter of the North Star State like Donna going to pour herself to watch the game? This mint-and-limeade fan favorite! Donna always goes the extra mile, so add Butterfly Pea Syrup to turn it all a festive purple for game day!

---

2 ounces white rum (can substitute vodka or gin)

½ ounce lemon juice

½ ounce lime juice

1 ½ ounces Butterfly Pea Syrup (page 14)

2 cups ice

10 to 15 mint leaves

½ ounce Creme de Mure (optional)

1 dehydrated lime wheel, for garnish

Blend all ingredients on high for 10 seconds. Empty into your glass of choice. The optional Creme de Mure adds an additional berry kick and reinforces the Minnesota purple color. Garnish with mint and a dehydrated lime wheel.

GHOSTFACERS TAKE MANHATTAN

When it comes to facing down the supernatural, few set out to make a name for themselves (let alone as literally) as did the Ghostfacers. Ed Zeddmore and Harry Spangler started by hyping up local ghostly legends online. But after a brush with the real thing (plus Sam and Dean Winchester), their ambitions grew into an attempt at becoming reality television ghost-hunting celebrities. Although they never quite made it to the "big time," these fame hunters repeatedly proved just as bold (and nutty) as this take on the big-time city cocktail. This version interrupts the usual program to replace the usual sweet vermouth with Amaro's brash, floral, and citrus buzz. The spicy rye base keeps this drink fired up, and a two-cherry garnish makes it ready for the spotlight!

---

2 ounces rye whiskey
1 ounce Amaro Montenegro
¼ ounce port wine
2 dashes orange bitters
3 dashes walnut bitters
2 cherries, for garnish

Stir all ingredients in a mixing glass. Strain into a chilled coupe or martini glass and garnish with a cherry or two.

GOOD BOY

Garth Fitzgerald (the Fourth) has always been a big puppy dog of a person—even before he got turned into a werewolf. But not even that transformation could really change this sweet-natured, helpful hunter. With Garth's tastes being equally sweet and simple, whether he's tagging along on a case or answering the call to be your alibi, he's probably going to reward himself with a treat like this one for being such a good boy. Like a milkshake with a bite, this concoction blends rich, creamy flavors with distinctive banana and chocolate liqueurs. Unlike dogs, werewolves can still enjoy chocolate.

1½ ounces vodka
½ ounce crème de cacao (dark)
¼ ounce lemon juice
3 ounces milk
Shaved dark chocolate, for garnish

BANANA CREAM:
2 ounces heavy cream
½ ounce banana liqueur
½ ounce Simple Syrup (page 13)

To make the banana cream, add heavy cream, banana liqueur, and Simple Syrup to an empty shaker. Dry-shake for 10 to 15 seconds or until lightly whipped and incorporated. You want a cream that is thick and pourable, but not fully whipped. Set aside until you're ready to build your cocktail.

Combine the vodka, crème de cacao, and lemon juice. Stir together and set aside. Pour milk into a separate container, followed by the cocktail mixture, and stir well. The acid from the lemon juice will begin the process of separating the milk curds from the whey. Strain the whole mixture using a coffee filter or cheesecloth—this will take a while, so be patient. Not only will this process clarify your cocktail visually, but it will remove many impurities and harsh flavors. Once the process has finished, discard the curds and transfer the clarified cocktail to an ice-filled shaker. Shake the cocktail and strain into a chilled coupe. Finish with a layer of your prepared banana cream, and top it all with shaved dark chocolate.

MEN OF LETTERS MIXOLOGY GUIDE

An elite and secretive society dedicated to the eradication of all that is unholy, unnatural, and undead, the Men of Letters are a class of "hunter" wholly unto themselves. The order's century-old origins are just as closely guarded as the privileged and proprietary spells and technological innovations their members have developed. Among the benefits enjoyed by fully initiated, blood-lineage members, the Men of Letters offer tremendous resources for investigation, protection, and comfort.

Upon the Brothers Winchester stepping into their inheritance of bloodline Men of Letters, they found themselves availed of significantly greater supplies and selection for their alcohol concoctions as well. Though the vast majority of the international order's accrued treasures shall not or cannot be made public, should you find yourself with a similarly robust bar, we now share some selections with which you can make good use of such an inheritance.

THE MILLIONAIRE

The joke associated with these drinks in their heyday was for a relatively common man to plea with the bartender to "make me a millionaire!" The feeling of richness offered in its flavors was surely a relief to people at the time, looking to escape both Prohibition and the Great Depression. One imagines a similar relief felt by Sam and Dean upon inheriting the Men of Letters estate: a mystically fortified home far finer than endless roadside motels, stores of hunters' resources and research, and an expertly stocked and curated parlor for gentlemen's alcohol appreciation. Should they have toasted the occasion with this selection, the brothers undoubtedly would have enjoyed the celebratory sensation of sweet, tart, and bold flavors.

1½ ounces dark rum
¾ ounce crème de mûre
¾ ounce peach brandy
1 ounce lime juice
1 dehydrated lime round, for garnish

Shake dark rum, crème de mûre, peach brandy, and lime together. Double-strain into a chilled coupe or martini glass and float a dehydrated lime round for garnish.

BRANDY CRUSTA

This Prohibition-era sidecar is the first cocktail in documented mixology to incorporate citrus fruits and thusly is the grandfather of citrus cocktails. And while Sam and Dean's grandfather Henry Winchester only spent a brief, stolen bit of time (travel) with his heirs, it allowed him to unlock the order's legacy for them. Much like the headquarters and resources of the Men of Letters, this beverage was extremely opulent for its time. The rich flavors of the cognac and curaçao are accented and perhaps outdone by the sweetness of maple and sugar, and ultimately the aroma and flourish of its elaborate garnish: a circular citrus peel along the entire rim. In hindsight, one could see it as a bold and unbroken line, much like the Winchesters themselves.

---

2 ounces cognac

½ ounce lemon juice

¼ ounce Rich Demerara Sugar Syrup (page 13)

¼ ounce curaçao

1 to 2 dashes Angostura bitters

1 orange peel, for garnish

Shake all ingredients and double-strain into a sugar-rimmed cocktail glass. Garnish with an orange peel that runs along the inside of the glass rim, leaving space for comfortable sipping.

LONDON MARTINI

While most of these selections are based on the American Men of Letters' traditions, it would be remiss to exclude a significant entry from across the pond. Just as Arthur Ketch arrived from the English chapter to impose its idea of order onto monsters (and hunters) in the states, he proved no less exacting in style and taste. To that end, this signature cocktail of course insists on London gin whose dryness borders on "brut." The thorough preparation creates a fragrant air. While sharp, bitter undertones ultimately balance out to provide a strong, elegant contender.

---

2 ounces London dry gin

½ ounce dry vermouth

½ ounce Lillet Blanc

2 dashes orange bitters

2 dashes grapefruit bitters

1 grapefruit zest, for garnish

Add gin, vermouth, Lillet, and bitters into a mixing glass and stir well. Strain into a chilled martini glass and garnish with grapefruit zest.

FATHER THOMPSON

An earlier iteration of this entry, a more traditional Trinidad Sour, was added to the order's repertoire in the earliest days of Angostura bitters, while they were still touted as a "medicinal" breakthrough. Claims of their restorative properties, however, did not bear out. This variation was named after Father Max Thompson, a Catholic priest among the Men of Letters' post-war roster whose experiments with developing a cure to demonic possession, conversely, proved genuine and successful. This sour substitutes Peychaud's and Sazerac, both originating in New Orleans, and marries these particular bitters and rye whiskey with brighter citrus and allspice sweetener. Some suggest the drink was renamed as a wink to New Orleans' own Catholic roots. Others claimed it was due to the bright red color evoking Father Thompson's more sanguine experiments.

---

1 ounce Peychaud's bitters
1 ounce falernum
¾ ounce fresh lemon juice
½ ounce Sazerac rye
1 lemon peel, for garnish

Shake all ingredients and double-strain into a chilled Nick and Nora glass, or a coupe. Garnish with a decorative lemon peel.

SMOKE, ON HIGH

The traditional Highball is a simple construct of whiskey and soda. However, such plain fare is unbefitting of a Man or Woman of Letters. A palate truly worthy of the order would surely prefer unique alteration. Here, the tart-sweet flavors of tonic and lime intermingle with the tang of fresh grapefruit, then soften and diffuse in soda water. The blend then tames the smoke of your finest scotch, echoing the smoke of demons vanquished by your same hand. Resultantly, the Men of Letters' methods once again sophisticate the simple and boorish into something refined and elevated.

---

2 ounces peated scotch
½ ounce lemon juice
½ ounce grapefruit juice
½ ounce tonic syrup
3 ounces club soda
1 grapefruit slice, for garnish

Shake the scotch, lemon juice, grapefruit juice, and tonic syrup and strain into an iced highball glass. Add the club soda and stir well. Garnish with a slice of grapefruit.

ADIEU DELPHINE

This particular entry in the Men of Letters mixology guide is named and dedicated in honor of a fallen agent. Delphine Seydoux was a French-born, decorated operative of the order. On her final mission, she successfully infiltrated a Nazi operation that had obtained powerful remains from the Arc of the Covenant. While Delphine did not survive her mission, she succeeded in it. In fitting memoriam, the French spirits here infiltrate the German base. St-Germain subtlety and sweetness hide a sharp lemon edge as all the flavors blend into the hearty, banana notes of the Hefeweizen.

---

1 ounce cognac
3.4 ounces St-Germain
½ ounce lemon juice
¼ ounce Lillet Blanc
2 to 3 ounces German Hefeweizen
1 dehydrated lemon wheel, for garnish

Shake cognac, St-Germain, lemon juice, and Lillet and strain into an ice filled collins or highball glass. Top with Hefeweizen and garnish with a dehydrated lemon wheel.

HOT MRS. BUTTERS RUM

Though fairly ruthless in their campaign to wipe out any and all supernatural threats to mankind, the American Men of Letters made a notable exception for their own housekeeper. Mrs. Butters may seem like a sweet older caretaker, but she's actually a fiercely protective wood nymph. And while many of the recipes in this section were creations or refinements tailored specifically for "her boys," Mrs. Butters herself loved few things as much as celebrating the holidays. This hot buttered rum recipe is as sweet and indulgent as its namesake. Its smooth, warming effects make this a perfect cold weather comfort; you'll feel like you're wrapped in hugs!

---

1 750-milliliter bottle of Jamaican rum

2½ sticks of butter (282 grams)

COCKTAIL

2 ounces brown butter–washed rum

¾ ounces Cinnamon Vanilla Syrup (page 14)

6 ounces boiling water

1 cinnamon stick, for garnish

First, we need to fat-wash our rum. Take 2½ sticks of room temperature, unsalted butter and cook over medium heat until perfectly browned and nutty. You're looking for a brown butter, not burnt, roughly 8 to 10 minutes. In a separate container, combine 1 bottle of rum and the brown butter. Using an immersion blender, or whisk, blend to combine and set aside to infuse for an hour or two. Transfer container to the freezer for a few hours or until the butter has risen and solidified at the top. Remove from the freezer and either remove the layer of fat or poke a hole in it and drain the mixture through cheesecloth. Using a funnel, return your brown butter-washed rum into its original bottle. Now you have a shelf stable flavor bomb of rum full of rich butterscotch notes, perfect for cocktail enhancement or just enjoyed by itself.

To prepare the cocktail, simply add 2 ounces of brown buttered rum to an Irish coffee mug with Cinnamon Vanilla Syrup and top with boiling water. Stir to combine and garnish with a cinnamon stick.

CREATURE COMFORTS

The key to survival is to know your enemy. Of course, as a hunter, there's enough lore for each type of monster to fill a book twice this size. But as we focus on the mixological arts, there's still plenty to learn about how cocktails can help combat all kinds of creeps and critters.

From sweet to sharp, from simple to death-defying, the recipes here are as wide-ranging and unique as the beasts and baddies they illuminate. But if pouring a glass can prepare you for some future fight? It's a tough job, but someone's got to do it.

* Cherubim Rank

SHAPESHIFTER FIZZ

Of all the creatures moving among us, the trickiest to identify might be shapeshifters. Unless they're rushed or sloppy enough to leave a pile of shed skin and teeth lying around after a makeover, you'd never know the person you're sharing drinks with is something inhuman. One reason may be that shapeshifters don't lash out on animal instinct. The Winchester brothers report encounters with completely peaceful shifters just trying to live normal human lives. So, whether you're looking to bond with one, are secretly a shapeshifter yourself, or get a gut feeling your date isn't who they say they are, this is your concoction. The flavors are creamy and fruity, but when the soda hits, the meringue undergoes its own transformation! As your date watches the dynamic drink in surprise, hit a sly "record" on your phone. Their one giveaway: A shifter's eyes flare on video.

---

2 ounces Midori

1 ounce heavy cream

2¾ ounces lime juice

¾ ounce Simple Syrup (page 13)

1 egg white

2 to 3 dashes orange flower water (or orange bitters)

2 ounces cold seltzer water

Lime zest, for garnish

Dry-shake the Midori, cream, lime, Simple Syrup, egg white, and orange flower water. Add ice, shake again, and double-strain into a collins glass. Top with soda water and watch the volume rise as the foamy head moves skyward. Finish the cocktail with microplaned lime zest for a fragrant garnish.

GHOST-PROOF MARGARITA

Ghosts, specters, revenants, poltergeists—there are almost as many types of undead souls terrorizing the living as there are grains of salt in a shaker. With so many vengeful spirits wreaking havoc, maybe the safest drink to make for yourself is this blended margarita? The sweet fruit flavors will keep you feeling lively, while an unbroken salt rim forms an uncrossable line to keep your drink safe from haunting hands. Add some spice with a Tajin rim as a fiery reminder to burn the ghost's remains once you've finished your drink.

---

2 ounces Reposado tequila

1 ounce fresh lime

1 ounce triple sec

¾ ounce agave syrup

1 to 1½ cups frozen mango (or frozen fruit of choice)

½ cup ice

½ teaspoon salt (optional . . . extra ghost protection)

1 lime, for garnish

2 slices of fresh mango, for garnish

2 tablespoons chamoy, for garnish

1 tablespoon Tajin, for garnish

Blend all ingredients until they reach a smooth consistency and all chunks are gone. Using chamoy and Tajin (a Mexican spice blend of chili, salt, and lime), rim a 12-ounce margarita glass, pour your cocktail, and garnish with a lime-and-mango skewer.

If hunting a shojo, remember they become visible to the fully intoxicated. Doubling the tequila for this recipe would make for a strong start.

BACON GRENADE

Less common, but potentially more dangerous and gruesome, wendigos and ghouls are two of the more flesh-hungry monsters on the prowl. Whether because of a wendigo's cannibal curse or the natural diet of the monstrous ghoul, if something's eating bodies nearby, this is the cocktail to (at least try to) relax with. The maple flavor creates a richly sweet complement to the umami bomb of the Bacon-Washed Bourbon. And with the spicy maple-bacon garnish, it's an excellent savory indulgence for you—or a great distraction to toss at a charging monster, hopefully giving you time to escape.

---

2 ounces Bacon-Washed Bourbon (page 15)

¼ ounce maple syrup

2 dashes orange bitters

2 dashes grapefruit bitters

Spicy Maple-Glazed Bacon (page 127), for garnish

Build in a double old-fashioned glass by combining Bacon-Washed Bourbon, maple syrup, and orange and grapefruit bitters. Stir, then garnish with a slice of Spicy Maple-Glazed Bacon.

FRESH BLOOD

One of the easiest ways to deal with a vampire (or, if you're really unlucky, a whole nest) is to incapacitate them with Dead Man's Blood. The stale stuff immediately sickens and weakens them. But unfortunately, many can smell the difference. Enter this helpful little elixir! Designed to mimic the way fresh blood smells to a vampire. This crimson cocktail not only appears like the real thing, but the fruity aromas are strong enough to mask any Dead Man's Blood you might mix in to knock that vampire down for the *count*. Plus, if you're an undercover bloodsucker yourself, you can enjoy the unspiked version. Its zesty and spicy flavors will keep you as sharp as old Nosferatu's fangs.

---

2 ounces Reposado tequila
1 ounce tomato juice
1 ounce lime juice
1 ounce orange juice
4 dashes Mexican hot sauce
2 ounces grapefruit soda
2 tablespoons salt, for garnish
1 fresh grapefruit wheel, for garnish
1 serrano pepper, for garnish

Shake tequila, tomato juice, lime juice, orange juice, and hot sauce with ice and strain into a salt-rimed highball, or collins, glass. Top with grapefruit soda. Give cocktail a gentle stir and garnish with a skewer of grapefruit and serrano pepper.

FULL MOON

A genuine favorite in pubs pouring for the werewolves of London, this mix supposedly pairs especially well with fresh meat. The drink, at least, can still be enjoyed by the less flea-ridden. Its botanical notes lend a scent of running through the wilds, while the cherry and raspberry elements create the reddish-purple tint of a changing moon. Cautious hunters make it until they can recognize the drink at a distance and arm themselves accordingly.

1½ ounces London dry gin
½ ounce crème de violette
½ ounce Luxardo maraschino liqueur
½ ounce crème de framboise
¾ ounce fresh lemon juice
1 maraschino cherry, for garnish
1 lemon peel, for garnish

Shake all ingredients and double-strain into a chilled cocktail glass. Garnish with a maraschino and a lemon twist.

SCOTTISH MULLED WINE

This age-old potion has become a traditional choice for Christmases, winter gatherings, and witches' covens from Scotland to Eastern Europe. (And, of course, the winter solstice rituals of Scottish witches like Rowena MacLeod, wherever they occur.) Whether prepared in a bowl or cauldron, the spiced wine punch draws its power and flavor from well-brewed ingredients. Season to taste. Stir and serve heated.

One 750-milliliter bottle medium-bodied wine

One 750-milliliter bottle tawny port

4 ounces Highland scotch

4 ounces Glayva or Drambuie

2 cinnamon sticks

2 tablespoons whole allspice berries

2 tablespoons whole cloves

2 tablespoons cardamom pods

¼ cup honey or brown sugar

¼ teaspoon freshly grated nutmeg

1 large orange sliced into rounds, for garnish

1 cinnamon stick, for garnish

Combine all ingredients (except the garnish) into a saucepan and simmer over medium-low/low heat (don't boil) for 30 minutes to an hour. Serve warm in 2 heatproof mugs and garnish with an orange slice and cinnamon stick.

LEVIATHAN SAZERAC

Lore claims Sazerac was the first cocktail created in America. This variation adds the bite of Peychaud's bitters and sharp anise aroma of absinthe to puncture the mescal, and your senses. As poured bitters get devoured into the sugar cube, then the larger concoction consumes and destroys the sugar—you see why hunters call it a Leviathan Sazerac after the first created monsters, known for devouring everything they come across.

---

1 sugar cube (1 teaspoon sugar)
4 dashes Peychaud's bitters
2 dashes orange bitters
1 teaspoon cold water
2 ounces mescal
¼ ounce absinthe, for rinse
1 lemon peel, for garnish

Place the sugar cube in a mixing glass. Add the Peychaud's, orange bitters (sugar should be saturated), and a splash of cold water. With your muddler, press and break down the sugar cube, working in circular motions to integrate the sugar into the solution. Add mescal and stir well to combine. Take a chilled rocks glass and give a spray or rinse with absinthe. Strain your cocktail from the mixing glass into the chilled and rinsed rocks glass and garnish with a lemon peel. Be sure to express the lemon oils over the top of your cocktail and rub the peel along the inside and outside of the rocks glass rim before placing it inside the cocktail.

TEDDY'S MEDICINE

Though Dean Winchester may have dismissed amaretto and Irish cream, this sweet and frothy mix is enjoyed by at least one sentient teddy bear brought to life and turned giant by a cursed wishing well! And just as it helped that bear (briefly) numb the pain of existential dread in a world of bleak news and endless pretend tea parties, two out of two teddy bear doctors say this medicine might be right for you.

---

1 crushed and powdered graham cracker, for garnish

2 ounces amaretto

1 ounce pineapple juice

1 ounce Irish cream

1 ounce Cinnamon Vanilla Syrup (page 14)

½ ounce crème de cacao

1 egg

2 to 4 ounces English or brown porter

Place 1 graham cracker in a sealed plastic zip-lock bag. Using a mallet, or blunt instrument, pound the cracker into a powder and set aside for garnish.

Dry-shake the amaretto, pineapple, Irish cream, Cinnamon Vanilla Syrup, crème de cacao, and egg. Add ice, shake, and strain into a chilled collins glass. Top with porter and garnish with powdered graham crackers.

STREGA COLLINS

Here's an important one to clear up for new hunters (especially as you're bound to spend plenty of time in bars, one way or another). Shtrigas are a form of witch that feed off human lifeforce—usually children—but plenty parts of the world call the same thing a "strega." Dangerous misunderstandings have occurred when hunters don't know "Strega" is also the name of a liqueur. So, familiarize yourself with this cordial and its mix of citrus and fennel flavors. Before you try your best witch-hunting tactics on some innocent barfly or confused liquor store clerk (like too many rookies before you).

1½ ounces gin or vodka
1 ounce Strega
¾ ounce lemon juice
4 to 6 ounces soda water
Lemon, for garnish

Shake gin, Strega, and lemon juice with ice and strain into a highball glass. Top with soda water. Garnish with a lemon.

THE FOUR HORSEMEN

When Sam Winchester destroyed the demon Lilith, unwittingly breaking the final seal to unleash Lucifer from Hell, he also set forth the Four Horsemen of the Apocalypse. Each one is so powerful, their influence can be felt on mankind from another plane. Once they were on Earth, each transformed all souls around them in their image. The following four drinks were inspired by these awesome beings.

FAMISHED MULE

To feel the touch of Famine is to hunger for more. His name usually refers to a desperation for food, but his influence makes mortals destructively ravenous for whatever they crave: pleasure, money, power . . . . Still, stoking literal hunger may be his favorite. Grapefruit and ginger, on the other hand, are often recommended to dieters for curbing appetites. So, this drink leverages their power to fend off Famine's pull—in a light and bright cocktail. Just stay on your toes. If you realize you're reaching for your fourth or fifth, Famine might have pulled you down a different path.

---

2 ounces Reposado tequila

1 ounce Giffard Crème de Pamplemousse (grapefruit liqueur)

2 ounces fresh grapefruit juice

½ ounce lime juice (or half a lime, juiced)

2 to 3 ounces ginger beer

1 dash Peychaud's bitters

1 dehydrated grapefruit wheel, for garnish

This is one time when it's perfectly fine to build your citrus-forward cocktail in the glass, or a copper mug. Add all the ingredients to your chosen glassware and give a good stir. Garnish with a dehydrated grapefruit wheel.

WHAT AILS YOU

When Pestilence creeps in, we often don't notice until the germs are already multiplying. And if it's brought by the Horseman, cold medicine alone won't cut it. But, alcohol kills germs, right? So, consider this a little all-in-one alternative medicine. The light and effervescent mix even has some soda water! When you're sick, you've got to stay hydrated.

---

2 ounces Aperol

¾ ounce Shrub (page 14)

1 ounce soda water

3 ounces champagne (like cava or prosecco)

1 strawberry trimmed, halved and skewered, for garnish

2 to 3 sage sprigs, for garnish

Add Aperol and Shrub to an ice-filled wineglass and top with soda water and champagne. Gently stir to combine and garnish with a strawberry skewer and sage sprigs positioned next to straw.

ALL-OUT WAR

The Horseman of War once described himself to Sam Winchester as "Jell-O shots at a party"—not a controlling force, but freeing humans to do what they want. But in traditional folklore, the cut-loose nectar of the gods was ambrosia. And since there are ages and occasions where folks might not take to Jell-O shots, this ambrosia recipe might be a more all-purpose party-starter. The creamy, orange-forward flavor makes a mixture so delectably drinkable that even Grandma might be busting loose before she knows what hit her.

---

1 ounce dark rum (like Goslings)
1 ounce pineapple juice
1 ounce orange juice
½ ounce maraschino liqueur
½ ounce triple sec
½ ounce coconut rum
1 toasted marshmallow, for garnish
1 fresh-cut cube of pineapple, for garnish
1 maraschino cherry, for garnish

Shake all ingredients with ice and strain into a hurricane glass filled with crushed or pebble ice. Garnish with a skewer of lightly toasted marshmallow, fresh pineapple, and a cherry.

PALE HORSE

Ancient Greeks referred to pomegranates as "the fruit of death." Some of the oldest hunter lore references Death himself harvesting some to add their tangy juice to his cocktails. Of course, in our modern era, the Horseman's tastes shifted to sodas that pair better with the artery-clogging foods he developed a taste for. (That is, until Dean Winchester nixed Death with his own scythe.) This piquant recipe offers a tart and timeless opportunity to have a safer type of near-Death experience.

---

2 ounces cognac
½ ounce lemon juice
1 ounce pomegranate molasses
1 egg white
4 to 6 pomegranate seeds

Dry-shake all ingredients, add ice, and shake again. Double-strain into a chilled coupe and garnish with some fresh pomegranate seeds. If you don't have any pomegranate seeds, you can use a skewered cherry instead.

RAISING HELL

Demons. The damned things are everywhere. These evil, human-possessing, soul-grubbing, black-smoke-escaping banes might just be the biggest plague on hunters (or, all humanity). If salt, holy water, or a devil's trap fails you against the big boys, don't give up hope—they've got other kinds of weaknesses. Remember we're talking about wholly corrupted souls—so one man's vice is another demon's virtue. And while, like angels, it takes a lot more alcohol to get a demon tipsy—unlike angels, they usually take that as a challenge. Learn how to serve up these extra-proof, demonically strong drinks, and you might soften them up enough to strike a bargain in your favor.

CRUZAN

SUMMONING BOWL

If you're planning to share a drink with a lost soul, or looking to summon up some company with an offer that's hard to refuse, this flaming brew casts a mighty spell. Like any true demon-summoning ritual, be precise with the elements. The results are powerful enough; this balance offers as much assurance as possible that it can be an enjoyable experience. Here, the juices and sweeteners round out the darker alcohols with natural and invigorating flavors. When all else is ready, ignite the flame and behold the powerful spell cast, and a bedeviled companion in its thrall.

---

2 ounces lime juice
2 ounces pineapple juice
1½ ounces Simple Syrup (page 13)
2 ounces orgeat
1 ounce falernum
2 ounces brandy
4 ounces gin
4 ounces lightly aged rum
2 cups crushed or pebble ice
½ lime, hollowed out, for garnish
1 sugar cube, for garnish
¼ ounce high-proof spirit (like 151), for garnish

Combine all ingredients into a blender and blend for 10 seconds. Pour the contents into a traditional scorpion bowl or small punch bowl. Garnish by floating a few orange slices. If using a scorpion bowl, place a 151-soaked sugar cube in the middle reservoir and set on fire. Or you can float a halved and hallowed piece of citrus as a bowl for your fire reservoir. Yields 4 servings.

DEVIL'S PUNCH

Let's get real. If one demon shows up, there's a good chance a bunch more are on their way. And once you've got a bunch of Hell-dwellers looking for fun, you're either the life of the party, or your death will be. This party punch uses the bright flavors of cherry liqueurs to create an immediate lure of sweetness, layers in more subtle alcohol (champagne and brandy) for strength, then brightens the whole affair with citrus and ginger beer. The result can please even the roughest crowds . . . as long as you make enough.

---

2 ounces maraschino liqueur
2 ounces Heering cherry liqueur
2 ounces brandy or cognac
2 cups ginger beer
One 750-milliliter bottle champagne
2 to 3 fresh orange slices, for garnish
1 maraschino cherry, for garnish

In a punch bowl or large pitcher, combine all ingredients and chill covered in the refrigerator overnight up to 24 hours. When ready to serve, ladle into an ice-filled tumbler or punch mug and garnish with fresh citrus slices and a cherry.

TRADER DICK'S

What can be said about Crowley that hasn't already been said by himself, or his countless enemies who despise him across Heaven, Earth, and all of Hell? Compared to far more powerful or ancient forces, this former middle-management crossroads demon ultimately proved far more sly, effective, and resilient than some of the most powerful beings in existence. He also betrayed and/or tried to murder practically everyone he ever knew.

As a spirit who spent a good couple of centuries tricking desperate people out of their souls and then staged a ruthless coup to become King of Hell, Crowley knew when his goals aligned with erstwhile enemies and would willingly help people like the Winchesters against evils, end times, or annihilating angels. Could it have been this tiki-style rich and fruity cocktail Crowley took a liking to that mellowed him out in the end? Or was its triple rum and blackberry liqueur–fueled heart the secret sauce of his more ruthless years on the rise? We'll likely never know, but perhaps this is the perfect drink for those who'd trade their souls to live long and conquer.

---

1 ounce aged rum

½ ounce lightly aged rum

½ ounce dark aged rum

½ ounce blackberry liqueur (like crème de mûre)

¾ ounce fresh lime juice

¾ ounce Rich Demerara Sugar Syrup **(page 13)**

2 to 3 blackberries, for garnish

3 to 4 mint sprigs, tops only, for garnish

Shake all ingredients with ice and double-strain into your tiki mug of choice filled with crushed or pebble ice. Garnish with fresh blackberries on a trident pick and a bouquet of fresh mint.

1881

HOT APPLE

Of all the beings of Hell, Lucifer gets a bad rap. Sure, he's been the force of temptation, demanded demons harvest human souls, and repeatedly tried to end the world, but we're talking about a former archangel here—of course he's got good qualities, too! And many of his underappreciated aspects are reflected in this particular cocktail. First and foremost, the dominant fiery and apple flavors (as he shall rightfully dominate all life) demonstrate that Ol' Scratch still has a sense of humor. The cloves and cinnamon add subtlety and complexity that prove he's no base or savage beast (unlike the endless horrors of Hell he'll one day unleash to tear human souls from their pathetically fragile bodies). And finally, his willingness to wait for this recipe to ripen into its perfect blend only goes to show his patience (which is a virtue—meaning Lucifer is, by definition, virtuous). Give in to one little taste of this alluring apple, and you'll see—not so bad after all.

---

4 apples, sliced (a sweet apple works best here)

One 750 milliliter bottle bourbon

2 cinnamon sticks

5 cloves

1 to 2 dried chile de arbol peppers

Slice and bake apples on a lined baking sheet at 400°F for 30 to 40 minutes, or until the apples begin to brown and caramelize. Transfer to a container and add your bourbon and spices, then set aside to infuse overnight, or for up to 2 weeks for a more intense flavor (for a subtler chili spice, remove the chili after the first day). When the infusion is ready, it should taste like cinnamon candy. Strain into a container or reuse the original bourbon bottle. Serve neat, on the rocks, or try in a cocktail, like an old-fashioned.

ICED RUBY

This ruby-red, coolly alluring concoction is likely to remind those who've met her of a particular demon. The Ruby that Sam and Dean Winchester became entangled with claimed to be a remorseful soul, trapped in the thrall of Hell. But her time aiding the brothers was an act, layering truth and deception as she manipulated Sam toward a destiny that included freeing Lucifer from Hell. This "ruby" is also far from what it seems. No simple, saccharine kids' snow cone—the flavors poured into the crushed-ice base are a blend of your finest vodka, sour stings of lemon juice, seductive fragrance of elderflower, and subtle but radiant watermelon. However, when this ruby's true nature hits, the surprise is a complex delight.

1½ ounces vodka
¾ ounce lemon juice
¾ ounce watermelon juice
½ ounce elderflower liqueur
½ ounce Aperol
1 lime wheel, for garnish
1 small watermelon wedge, for garnish

Shake vodka, lemon juice, watermelon juice, elderflower, and Aperol with ice and strain into a double old-fashioned glass over a dome of crushed ice. Garnish with a fresh watermelon wedge and lime wheel.

GOD SAID NO

He may be no demon, but when the angel Castiel set out to get drunk, he "found a liquor store—and drank it." His combinations and epic consumption that night became legendary even in Hell, and is commemorated here. It might not take a looming Apocalypse, or a literal and explicit rejection from God to summon you to this recipe. But whatever you're looking to forget, you might still want to say your prayers first.

Usually, this would be the place to talk about what flavors to expect or something. But this is mostly an alcohol onslaught, so let's just say, "don't make any plans for tomorrow."

½ ounce white rum
½ ounce mescal
½ ounce Luxardo maraschino liqueur
½ ounce amaretto
¾ ounce lime juice
¾ ounce Simple Syrup (page 13)
1 to 2 ounces ginger beer
1 lime wheel, for garnish

Shake rum, mescal, maraschino liqueur, amaretto, lime juice, and Simple Syrup. Strain into an ice-filled pint glass and top with ginger beer. Give a stir and garnish with a lime wheel.

SMOKE AND SCARLET

While "smoky spirits" could describe any demons on the go, few managed to escape expert hunters like the Winchesters as often as Abaddon. One of the first human souls subjected to demonic transformation in Hell, she had thousands of years to hone her survival skills. And though Abaddon may not have succeeded in seizing Lucifer's empty throne for herself, this commanding she-devil easily persuaded a large swath of the infernal realm to lick her boots and fetch her drinks. This pour reflects her colorful presence, smoking air, bitter heart, and enduring bite.

1½ ounces peated scotch
¾ ounce Amaro Averna
¾ ounce Campari

1 grapefruit peel, for garnish (or 1 orange peel)

Combine all ingredients into an ice-filled double old-fashioned glass and stir. Garnish with a grapefruit peel. Be sure to express the skin's oils over the cocktail and rub the oily flesh along the rim of the glass.

DARKNESS AND STORMY

In the beginning, there was God. And he said, "Let there be light."

Or so we were told. But for light to debut in that earliest existence, it means God was there, not alone, but with The Darkness. Those two beings, we've come to learn, were like siblings. But as brother and sister, as much as they were bonded, they also had epic fights. After God locked The Darkness outside of reality for millions of years, she returned confused, angry, and intent on destroying God's creation. "Amara" (as she'd come to be known on Earth) had simple intentions. She aimed to consume the souls of humans, demons, and anything else that crossed her path until she was strong enough to return all of creation to the black void of oblivion. While she ultimately found balance, consider this an offering to the other original being. Just as simple and pure as The Darkness itself, this timeless original might require several consumptions to reach full strength. But soon enough, it will lead anyone into oblivion.

---

2 to 3 ounces ginger beer

½ ounce grenadine (or ½ ounce Campari for a bitter kick)

2 ounces dark rum

1 dehydrated lime wheel, for garnish

Fill a highball glass with ice. Add ginger beer and grenadine (or Campari) and stir to combine. Add rum, then garnish with a dehydrated lime wheel.

BLACK EYE MAI TAI

One giant load of booze in a glass, coming up. This twist on the tiki bar classic mai tai gets the usual fruit juice the hell out of there in favor of a few simple cocktail sweeteners and a dash of lime to keep that island appeal—and make room for more liquor! The extra-proof will knock the knees out of most black-eyed body-jackers. Mere mortals might want to sip rather than gulp this one down, lest you wake up with black eyes of your own.

---

3 ounces dark rum

1 ounce light rum

¼ ounce triple sec

¼ ounce orgeat

¼ ounce Demerara Sugar Syrup (page 13)

¼ ounce lime

1 small wedge of pineapple, for garnish

1 maraschino cherry, for garnish

Shake all ingredients and strain into a tiki tumbler or double old-fashioned glass filled with crushed or pebble ice. Garnish with a pineapple slice and a cherry.

ENTERTAINING ANGELS

Of course, there are all manner of beings in Heaven and Earth whose drinks should go untouched by alcohol when you're playing host (in any sense of the word). If an angel is using someone as their earthly vessel, not only do most turn their noses up at human vices, but booze has essentially no effect on them. (And "waste not, want not," right?) Other selections here are tried-and-true favorites for younger guests – as hunters should be prepared when keeping kids safe from the current monster of the week. The good news is most of these recipes also taste just as delightful with a particular hooch-injection to get you through any exhausting situations.

DEPARTMENT of
FEDERAL BUREAU OF INVESTIGATION
SPECIAL AGENT
MENT of INVESTIGATION

HEAVEN SENT

The angel Castiel first made himself known by rescuing Dean Winchester's soul from Hell. In the years and countless averted end times since, he's freed the souls of Purgatory, become a new leader of Heaven, lost his angelic grace, played host to Lucifer, died, and was resurrected (more than once). But among the biblically epic events, Castiel came to see his own journey as one toward love. Human feelings were confusing, and studying the pizza man sure didn't clear anything up. But aiding the Winchesters, and his bond with Dean especially, slowly awakened him to a depth of feeling, understanding, and caring he'd never known. In the end, his concern wasn't for the machinations of Heaven or Hell. It was for the simple joys and emotional connections here on Earth. So, enjoy earth's natural sweetness, fruit juices, in a confection that (like Castiel) becomes endlessly sweet. With bubbles rising to the heavens, it's the taste of a pineapple creamsicle that really spreads its wings. Share one with the person you love. Pairs perfectly with a burger.

---

4 ounces pineapple juice
¾ ounce lime juice
¾ ounce Simple Syrup (page 13)
1 ounce cream
2 to 3 ounces cold seltzer water
1 small wedge of pineapple, for garnish
2 pineapple leaves, for garnish

Combine pineapple juice, lime juice, Simple Syrup, and cream in a shaker and give a hard shake. Strain into an ice-filled collins glass and top with soda. Garnish with fresh pineapple and a couple of its leaves.

HOLY TRICKSTER

One of the hardest heavenly creatures to pin down, the archangel Gabriel reinvented himself as the Trickster demigod and Norse deity Loki (not to mention his countless disguises, pocket realities, and faked deaths). But whether he was running from Heavenly infighting, joining human rebels in an Apocalypse, faking alien abductions, or trapping the Winchesters in their guilty-pleasure TV favorites, one thing usually motivated Gabriel above all else—to keep the good times going. And his delightfully mercurial beverage can transform just as easily! Its flavors keep pulling the rug out from under you—sweetness one minute, minty or sour the next. When you need to satisfy your Trickster's sweet tooth, substitute ginger ale for soda water. Or, if you've lost your grace and feel the call for alcohol, manifest some beer to top it off instead! Any combination will be just as playful and effervescent as this former Host of Heaven.

¾ ounce lemon juice
¾ ounce Simple Syrup (page 13)
8 to 10 mint leaves
¼ cup any fresh berries or melon
2 ounces seltzer water, ginger ale, or ginger beer

Combine lemon juice, Simple Syrup, mint, and chosen fruit. Give a hard shake, double-strain into an ice-filled double old-fashioned glass, and top with desired soda.

CAGED MICHAEL

Stewing on his resentment of his brother Lucifer, then trapped in a cage with him as anger and madness seeped in, the archangel Michael is an epic reminder of how letting something simmer for too long can ratchet up the bitterness to biblical proportions. So just as Michael started as a sweetly devoted servant, this complexly flavored iced tea builds off honey and molasses underpinnings. The ginger and lemon add a radiant brightness. But its ultimate bitterness will depend on how long you leave the tea trapped in its boiling inferno.

---

4 cups water
1 black tea bag
¼ cup Ginger Honey Syrup (page 14)
¼ cup pomegranate molasses
3 to 4 mint sprigs, tops only, for garnish
1 fresh slice of lemon, for garnish

Boil your water and remove from heat to steep your tea, 5 to 10 minutes. Remove bag and stir in Ginger Honey Syrup and pomegranate molasses. Increasing the Ginger Honey Syrup will increase the sweetness. Serve over ice with a bouquet of mint and a lemon slice.

CUCUMBER GIMLET

Raphael wanted to keep things simple. The archangel believed in following God's plan. His brothers Michael and Lucifer should battle on Earth to kickstart the Apocalypse. Of course, for all his trouble, Raphael was sent to his own personal End Times by a powered up Castiel.

So, when you feel the urge to keep it simple—don't end the world. Stir up this quick and easy relaxer instead. It's tidy, tart, and effervescent.

---

5 to 6 cucumber slices
1 ounce lime juice
1 ounce fresh Simple Syrup (page 13)
3 ounces water
1 fresh cucumber ribbon, for garnish

Add cucumbers, lime juice, and Simple Syrup to a large shaking tin and muddle. Add water and ice and give a good hard shake. Double-strain into a chilled cocktail glass. Peel a cucumber from top to bottom using a Y-peeler to create the garnish.

FOR A NONANGELIC EXPERIENCE...

Sub out the soda for 2 ounces of gin or vodka.

SIP OF EDEN

According to angelic lore, the only true peace in human history was back in the Garden of Eden. Sadly for us, Eden's guardian angel, Gadreel, got played for a sucker by his big brother Lucifer. Gadreel, of course, tried to redeem himself—using Sam Winchester as his vessel and eventually returning fellow newly fallen angels to Heaven where they belong. But his real wish was an impossible one—to return our world to the Garden. But you can enjoy a taste of that dream with this simple, herbal refresher. Mix with soda water for a tart virgin spritz, or with ginger beer for a sweet-and-sour mock mule. Best enjoyed in peace (clothing optional).

---

4 ounces Shrub (page 14)
4 ounces soda water (or ginger beer for a mock mule)
1 strawberry, sliced, for garnish

Add Shrub to an ice-filled wineglass, top with soda, and stir to combine. Garnish with fanned strawberry slices on a garnish pick.

MELONTRON

Metatron may be best remembered as a surprisingly wily, shockingly effective manipulator—especially for an angel. This former Scribe of God took the loss of his prestigious job and his place in Heaven so poorly that he clipped all his brothers' wings to crash them down to Earth. Metatron rebuilt Heaven, appointed himself "new God," and began amassing followers on Earth. He's fooled and bested the Winchesters, Castiel, and countless angels again and again. But despite his long and notorious list of accomplishments, he really spends most of his time reading. Whether the ancient secret rituals of the Angel Tablet, the arcane spells of the Demon Tablet, or just the next Chuck Shurley *Supernatural* "novel," this bookish jerk makes a convincing argument that knowledge is power.

So behold, in this sacred text, the preferred sipping for those similarly keeping their mind sharp and pages turning! Lime purportedly stimulates the mind, while fresh mint is found to help engage memory and creativity. (The watermelon just makes plotting your revenge all the sweeter.)

---

1 ounce lime juice
1 ounce Simple Syrup (page 13)
10 to 12 mint leaves
½ cup fresh watermelon juice
2 to 4 ounces soda water
1 slice watermelon, for garnish
3 to 4 mint sprigs, tops only, for garnish

In a highball glass, add your lime juice, Simple Syrup, and mint and give a gentle muddle. Add ice, watermelon juice, and soda water and stir to combine. Garnish with a healthy bouquet of mint and a slice of watermelon.

SWEET HEARTS

Big, simple, and sweet. Those words could describe the enthusiastically affectionate Cupids—or the flavor in this blended, earthly concoction the love angels themselves would be quite fond of. The vibrant pink color and sudden chills you'll get from this virgin practically do half the work of the chubby cherubs' arrows. Meanwhile, the fruity goodness from real strawberries and orange juice will keep your heart healthy for the next time a Cupid really does have you in its sights!

---

16 ounces frozen strawberries (or fruit of choice)

¼ cup lime juice

¼ cup agave syrup

¼ cup fresh orange juice

¼ cup water

½ cup ice

1 fresh lime wheel, for garnish

1 fresh strawberry, for garnish

Blend all ingredients together and transfer into a salt-rimmed margarita glass. Garnish with a lime wheel and fresh strawberry.

CHOCOLATE SURPRISE

When you need to get some actual nutrition into kids under your care, this blended concoction delivers the goods while tasting great. The spices add flavor and richness to this super-simple mix, while the natural and satisfying banana-and-milk combo turns into a total treat with just a bit of chocolate syrup. The end result is a hit with even the pickiest palates—if your little one refuses to enjoy it, grab a mirror to check if they've been swapped out by a changeling waiting to feed on you instead. Surprise!

---

1 frozen banana
1½ cup milk
1 teaspoon cinnamon
1 ounce chocolate syrup
3 tablespoons whipped cream, for garnish
2 teaspoons grated chocolate, for garnish

Blend all ingredients and serve in a chilled sundae glass. Garnish with whipped cream and chocolate shavings.

TA-DA!

This one's for a different type of little angel. Whether you've got kids of your own or have to keep a couple rug-rats' minds off some ravenous monster hunting them, dazzle their tiny brains and taste buds with this colorful "magical" cooler. Sweet fruit juices and bubbling soda are always a hit with kiddos. But when the deep blue ice hits the citric acid, they'll love watching the drink transform in colorful swirls that ultimately create a purple treat. Time it right, and the process might distract them long enough for you to dispatch that pesky boogeyman before they know it's here!

---

4 cups water

1 cup dried butterfly pea flowers

½ ounce fresh orange juice

½ ounce pineapple juice

6 to 8 ounces grapefruit soda (such as Squirt)

1 fresh orange slice or small pineapple wedge, for garnish

For the ice, bring 4 cups of water to a boil, then turn off heat. Add hot water to 1 cup of dried butterfly pea flowers and steep for 2 to 4 minutes. Let cool and strain into an ice mold. Transfer to the freezer.

In a clear pint glass, or other clear cup of choice, add the blue ice and juices and top with soda. Stir and watch the drink turn purple as the citric acid from the soda and juices hit the ice. Garnish with an orange slice or fresh pineapple.

HAIR OF THE HELLHOUND

Long, rough nights are pretty much a guarantee for any hunter. But if you do the job right, that sun is still going to come up in the morning—and way too many shabby motels don't spring for the blackout curtains. So, after that rude awakening, it helps to remember there's usually a bar that opens for breakfast. Don't try to recover with a greasy pork sandwich. If you need a hangover cure, a little "hair of the dog that bit you" or just a job-well-done drink since you were too tired to celebrate last night, here are a few tried-and-true favorites in every hunter's a.m. arsenal.

BLOODY MARY

The Bloody Mary is both a quintessential day-starter cocktail and quintessential American ghost lore. In both cases, there are so many conflicting accounts of its origin that we'll likely never know which is the real deal. Sam and Dean Winchester claim to have lured and destroyed a genuine "Bloody Mary" summoned spirit. But with chilling accounts of mirror-bound specters answering that call at slumber parties or high school dares all across the country, there might be more than one ghoulish girl responding to that name. Similarly, call for Bloody Mary, the drink, and you might get one of countless variations. But if you choose to manifest one for yourself, this recipe delivers the classic spiced and zesty flavor—with a small secret in its unique rosemary infusion.

Of course, if you'd rather leave the mixing to a bartender, double-check that there are no mirrors hanging around—and never order more than twice.

---

2 ounces vodka

1 to 2 sprigs fresh rosemary

4 ounces tomato juice

¼ ounce lemon juice

¼ ounce lime juice

¼ ounce Maggi liquid seasoning (or Worcestershire sauce)

½ teaspoon horseradish

1, 2, or 20 dashes of your favorite hot sauce

½ teaspoon spice blend

1 to 2 sprigs fresh rosemary, for garnish

1 celery stick, for garnish

1 to 2 pickled vegetables of choice, for garnish

SPICE BLEND:

1 teaspoon celery salt

1 teaspoon freshly ground pepper

1 teaspoon sumac

1 teaspoon garlic powder

1 teaspoon onion powder

1 teaspoon cayenne

Start by infusing your vodka using 1 or 2 fresh sprigs of rosemary. This can be done in a separate container or straight in the bottle. Let sit for 2 hours or days in advance for maximum extraction.

Create your Spice Blend. Build your cocktail in a shaker and give a quick shake to combine. Strain over fresh ice in a pint glass; fine-strain for less grit. Garnish with a sprig of rosemary, trimmed celery stick, and your favorite pickled veg on a pick. Or throw a whole burger on the thing. Your drink—garnish as much or as little as you'd like.

MICHELADA

For a lighter pick, the Michelada makes a heck of a hangover helper. With less of the "shotgun of spices" that comes in the traditional Bloody Mary, this morning mender is easier to enjoy on a second, third, or even fourth round. (Whether you're swapping stories, digging through lore, or just reading obits for the next lead.)

---

2 tablespoons chamoy, for garnish
1 to 2 tablespoons Tajin, for garnish
¾ ounce fresh lime juice
¼ ounce Maggi liquid seasoning (or Worcestershire sauce)
2 ounces Clamato, or plain tomato juice
6 ounces lager of choice
2 dashes hot sauce (optional)
1 fresh lime wheel, for garnish

Using 2 small plates, pour some chamoy in one and Tajin in another. Take a pint glass and roll the rim in the chamoy, then again in the Tajin for a perfectly spicy rim.

In a large mixing tin, add lime, Maggi, Clamato, hot sauce (if using) and lager. Stir to combine, and transfer to your rimmed pint glass. Garnish with a lime and enjoy.

CORPSE REVIVER

Whether you need a bold and vibrantly tart cocktail to brighten your day, or you find yourself resurrecting the dead in need of information, this is the voodoo for you. As colorful in appearance as it is in its blend of fruit and floral flavors, this variation on the Corpse Reviver is calibrated to stimulate the mind (even one that's been rotting for a bit). There are numerous ways to raise a zombie, of course. Witchcraft, necromancy, demonic summoning—whatever your method, zombies are usually worse than groggy upon "waking up." So, make enough to share, and you'll both feel sharper and more like your old selves again.

¾ ounce hibiscus-infused gin

¼ ounce absinthe, for rinse

¾ ounce curaçao

¾ ounce Lillet Blanc

½ ounce lemon juice

¼ ounce maraschino liqueur

1 fresh lemon peel, for garnish

Combine gin with dried hibiscus flowers—¼ cup, or ½ cup for a full-bottle infusion—and age for 2 hours up to a few days before straining into a container or the original bottle.

Spray or rinse a chilled coupe with absinthe and set aside. Shake gin, curaçao, Lillet Blanc, lemon juice, and maraschino and double-strain into chilled absinthe-rinsed cocktail glass. Garnish with a lemon twist.

If you want to infuse a whole bottle of vodka with rosemary flavor, use 4 to 6 sprigs instead.

ESPRESSO BACON-TINI

Unfortunately for the blue-collar hunters, sometimes you're just plain stuck in a spot that doesn't have breakfast—only "brunch." For any Dean Winchester types, here's a fancy little Godsend. Booze, espresso (coffee), and bacon all in one? Hey, maybe there's something to this thing called "brunch" after all.

---

2 ounces Bacon-Washed Bourbon (page 15)

1 ounce coffee liqueur, such as Mr. Black, or strong cold brew

Maple cream (below)

1 teaspoon finely minced bacon, for garnish

MAPLE CREAM:

2 ounces heavy whipping cream

½ ounce maple syrup (use the good stuff)

For the maple cream, dry-shake the heavy whipping cream and the maple syrup for 10 to 15 seconds, looking for a light whip. Can be made ahead and stored in the refrigerator until needed.

Shake Bacon-Washed Bourbon and strong cold brew together and strain into a chilled coupe or martini glass. Gently lay the maple cream on top and garnish with finely minced bacon bits.

CARAJILLO

This Spanish coffee cocktail offers two perks in one. The name itself means "courage." In addition to it providing a hefty dose of caffeine, lore claims these precise ingredients can work as a fortifying potion when the drinker focuses their mind on their fearsome task at hand. Carajillo likely doesn't pack enough mystical power to overcome supernaturally induced terrors (such as ghost sickness, which reduced even Dean Winchester to a state of hysterical panic). But several hunters have found it helpful when they know a case will force them to confront personal phobias (e.g. Sam Winchester and his fear of clowns).

---

2 ounces Licor 43
½ ounce mescal
2 ounces chilled espresso
1 fresh orange peel, for garnish

Shake Licor 43, mescal, and espresso with ice and strain into an ice-filled double old-fashioned glass. Garnish with a fresh orange peel, making sure to express the oils over the cocktail and rub along the rim before garnishing the cocktail.

TRIP TO THE GARDEN

Finally, for one wanting a refreshing, rejuvenating morning beverage, consider this recipe, supposedly refined by the angel Serafina for her love, Adam. (Yes, that Adam. As in, "the first dude.") With angelic grace and a fondness for the new age and homeopathic outlook, this heavenly host kept her man alive for more than 300,000 years—so she must be doing something right. Let the tastes of fresh fruits and the eldest of flowers transport you back to the Garden of Eden. (Without any apples—or, more accurately, quince—leaving a bitter taste in your mouth.)

---

2 ounces fresh watermelon juice
½ ounce lime juice
1 ounce elderflower liqueur
2 dashes Angostura bitters
4 ounces prosecco (or brut champagne)
2 to 3 watermelon balls, for garnish

Shake watermelon juice, lime juice, elderflower liqueur, and Angostura and strain into a champagne glass. Top with prosecco. Use a melon baller or small spoon to create melon balls. Skewer them and garnish.

ROAD RATIONS

Hunters can't live on drinking alone. (Though plenty have tried it.) And at some point, we all find ourselves as the only living soul in a ghost town, or barricaded indoors against a horde of zombies or werewolves or some other damned thing until morning or a miracle saves us. Point is, there'll come a day when we all have to face our fears . . . and COOK.

Collected here are a few chosen recipes that cover all occasions. So, with any luck, you'll be prepared for anything. Like hunting, it'll take fortitude, and it might get a little messy. But the end results are so delicious, so irresistible, that if somebody around isn't tempted by them, you're probably looking at some kind of creature waiting to put you on the menu.

PIG IN A POKE

This breakfast special is such a taste sensation, some choose to eat it every single morning, again and again and again. In Dean Winchester's case, that was because he didn't realize he and his brother were trapped in a time loop by the Trickster (née Gabriel). But for others, the elbow grease (plus . . . regular grease) required for these sweet and savory day-starters is well worth it when it means being stocked up on something to stomp down a week's worth of hunter hangovers. Might not be part of the most balanced breakfast, but you only live once! (Unless you're in a murderous time loop.)

---

12 skewers

12 breakfast sausage links

2 cups all-purpose flour

2 cups buttermilk (add another ½ cup for a thinner pancake batter)

2 tablespoons sugar

2 teaspoons baking powder

1 teaspoon baking soda

½ teaspoon salt

2 large eggs

1 quart peanut or vegetable oil for frying

MAPLE MUSTARD SAUCE:

4 ounces maple syrup

2 ounces Dijon mustard (or stone-ground)

2 ounces yellow mustard

Start by soaking skewers in warm water and cooking the sausages until they are cooked through.

For your batter, combine all dry ingredients and wet ingredients separately. Slowly combine the wet into the dry and let sit for a few minutes. If the batter is too thick, add a little more buttermilk to thin it out. Prep the sausages by rolling them in a little flour before skewering them. Add the batter to your large mixing tin or a pint glass. Using a candy thermometer, heat oil to 350°F (177°C). Either a tall, narrow saucepan or shallow-frying in a cast-iron pan will work, but make sure to trim your skewers so they fit inside the pan. Carefully place the battered "pigs" into the oil, slowly giving them a gentle turn in the oil before releasing them to fry (this ensures a nice shape). Fry for 2 to 5 minutes, until light golden-brown. Using tongs, carefully remove from oil and place on a wire rack, or paper towels, to quickly dry and cool before plating.

Serve with maple mustard sauce, or coat in powdered sugar and dip in your favorite maple syrup—the choice is yours.

QUESO TO DIE FOR

Most of you reading this haven't had to face Death—at least not in the literal sense. But according to the Winchesters, the Horseman had a serious soft spot for rich, indulgent modern food. On a few occasions, they supposedly managed to bribe and negotiate with the head-honcho Reaper himself by feeding that hunger, including once with a Tex-Mex platter centered around queso. So, when you need to impress, implore, or impose—why not use the robust and flavorful cheese dip that was irresistible even to Death himself?

---

2 tablespoons neutral oil

1 small onion, diced fine

1 teaspoon salt

3 cloves garlic, minced

1 tomato, diced fine

¼ to ½ cup drained and diced pickled jalapeños

1 cup milk

2 cups American cheese

2 cups Monterey Jack cheese

2 cups Queso Oaxaca (can substitute another melty cheese like Havarti or Muenster or add 2 more cups of Monterey Jack)

¼ cup chopped cilantro

¼ cup chopped chives (optional)

Place oil in a medium saucepan and heat over medium heat until hot. Add onion and season with salt. Stir and cook until soft. Add garlic and cook for 2 to 3 minutes before adding tomato and jalapeño. Cook for another 2 to 3 minutes, stirring until softened and liquid has sweated out. Add milk, followed by your cheeses—stir in cheese in batches. Once all your cheese is integrated, continue to stir until you reach a silky-smooth consistency. Taste for seasoning, adding more salt if needed, and stir in cilantro or chives before serving. Serve with your favorite chips, or pour them on for quick and easy nachos.

DISCLAIMER: As the original, cosmic Death has since died and been replaced by a promoted Reaper, we do not guarantee similar bargaining results.

WINCHESTER
JOHN
TYPE AB
NON-RELIGIOUS

JOHN WINCHESTER'S KITCHEN SINK STEW

John Winchester's approach to hunting was pretty much: find the problem, then beat and burn the hell out of it. Turns out that was basically his approach to a cold or flu, too. His boys must've found it helpful, because they continued the tradition, making their dad's "Kitchen Sink Stew" as jam-packed and spicy as they could with whatever was on hand when the other fell under the weather. (Even if from unnatural causes.) So, you can take some liberties here and still honor the Winchester spirit. Just keep it loaded with every plant you've got, and spice it up as hot as your patient can handle. Or, why not cook up a big pot to wipe any microscopic monsters out of your system before they get the chance to wreak havoc in the first place?

---

2 tablespoons vegetable oil
Salt to taste
Pepper to taste
2 large carrots, diced
1 medium onion, diced
2 celery stalks, diced
1 cup cremini mushrooms, sliced
1 leek, halved and chopped
6 cloves garlic, minced
1½ pounds boneless, skinless chicken thighs
1½ teaspoons cayenne
2 sprigs thyme
2 sprigs rosemary
1½ quarts chicken stock
3 to 4 ounces Parmesan, cut into cubes
1 cup orzo
1 cup spinach, chopped
1 teaspoon parsley, chopped, for garnish

Heat oil in a stockpot over medium heat. Add salt, pepper, carrots, onion, celery, and mushrooms, stirring and cooking until translucent. Add leeks and garlic and cook for another 2 minutes. Season thighs with salt and pepper and add to the pot with cayenne, thyme, and rosemary. Cook for about 2 to 3 minutes, flipping chicken halfway through.

When the flesh of the chicken begins to whiten, add 1 quart of chicken stock and bring to a boil, then reduce to a simmer, uncovered for about 30 minutes. At this time, add the cubed Parmesan. You can also add the rind, which will be discarded later. Once the chicken is tender and cooked through, remove and discard the thyme, rosemary, and Parmesan rind. The rest of the Parmesan will dissolve into the broth. Using tongs, remove the chicken to a cutting board and let cool before shredding the meat using two forks.

Return chicken to the pot and stir in the orzo, along with the rest of the stock, about 1½ cups, and chopped spinach. Bring to a boil and reduce to a simmer, then cook for another 15 to 20 minutes, or until pasta is cooked through. Turn off heat and let cool for 5 minutes. Taste for seasoning and serve. Garnish with freshly chopped parsley. Yields 6 servings.

HEALTH QUAKE SALAD SHAKE

Hey—life can't only be about chili cheese fries and bottomless cocktails. The Reapers are out there. Let's not hurry them up too much. Luckily, this revised take on grab-and-go salads from Patriot Burger amps up the quality and healthy satisfaction. Stack your fresh-cut vegetables in separate layers to keep your crisp ingredients safely above the ripe and juicy tomatoes, and to maintain maximum distinct flavors. The pan-seared salmon and seasoned chickpeas pack enough protein and energy to keep you tracking demons, witches, and poltergeists all day. The all-natural, creamy zest of avocado pesto dressing brings it all together in a light but delightful glaze, when you're ready. Just shake it up, baby.

CRISPY CHICKPEAS:

One 15½-ounce can chickpeas

1 tablespoon olive oil

¼ teaspoon salt

¼ teaspoon fresh cracked pepper

½ teaspoon garlic powder

¼ teaspoon smoked paprika

AVOCADO PESTO DRESSING:

½ medium Hass avocado

2 cups packed basil

½ cup packed mint

½ cup grated Parmesan

½ cup extra-virgin olive oil

⅓ cup water

1 lemon, juiced

⅓ cup raw pistachios

2 cloves garlic

2 tablespoons extra-virgin olive oil

Salt and pepper to taste

SALAD:

4 to 5 ounces cooked salmon

½ cup tomatoes

1 cup kale

¼ cup red onion

½ cup corn

¼ cup shredded carrots

¼ cup crispy chickpeas

To make the crispy chickpeas, drain, rinse, and dry the chickpeas on a towel to remove moisture. Toss with oil and spices and spread on a rimmed baking sheet at 450°F (233°C) for 20 to 25 minutes, or until crispy. Set aside.

For the dressing, pulse ingredients together in a blender, or with an immersion blender. Season with salt and pepper to taste and set aside.

Pan-sear salmon over medium heat to desired doneness and set aside to cool. Once cooled, slice into bite-sized pieces and set aside. In a 32-ounce deli container, or cup with lid, layer your salad starting with tomatoes, kale, red onion, corn, salmon, carrots, and dressing. Top with chickpeas, leaving enough room to combine all ingredients. Shake and enjoy.

SPICY MAPLE-GLAZED BACON

Growing up, the Winchester brothers never stayed put in a school long enough to learn about the food groups. But they would've sworn at least two of the groups were bacon. You've got to give it to them—there's almost nowhere it doesn't make a meal better! On a burger? Absolutely. In a cookie? Next-level. Breakfast? Why is that even a question—you can't have breakfast without bacon. And while bacon is always good, homemade spicy maple bacon is always better. A little quick work adds layers of deep sweetness and a lightly spicy kick to some thick-cut bacon's natural rich and savory satisfaction.

---

12 ounces smoky bacon

3 ounces good-quality real maple syrup

1 teaspoon ground chile de arbol (or cayenne for a spicier kick)

½ teaspoon ground black pepper

Preheat the oven to 400°F (205°C). Place bacon on a sheet pan with a wire rack in the oven for 20 minutes. Meanwhile, in a small bowl, combine the maple syrup, chile de arbol, and pepper to create the glaze.

Remove bacon from the oven and glaze your bacon on both sides using a brush or spoon. Be sure to drain the grease from the pan and transfer bacon to a clean rack before glazing. Let the bacon cool so the glaze can set. Enjoy.

WASTE NOT; WANT NOT!

Eke out all the deliciousness your bacon has to offer by reserving the bacon grease for making Bacon-Washed Bourbon (page 8).

BOBBY'S HUNTER CHILI

For any folks who are hunters in the other sense of the word, carve out a little of what you bag for this time-tested, red-blooded, backwoods chili. Bobby Singer would be the first to say he's no gourmet chef. But after more than your share of decades messing around with the same recipe, even an idjit stumbles onto something special. And this isn't city-boy chili with beans and tofu. It's meat, spice, and even a little beer. Then some more meat for good measure. For folks who don't keep a deep freezer stocked full of fresh game, grocery store substitutions work just fine. (But then, can you really call yourself a hunter?)

---

1 large onion, diced

3 hatch chiles, chopped (or Anaheim or other mild chili)

2 jalapeños, chopped (remove the seeds to decrease the heat level)

2 dried pasilla peppers

1 red bell pepper, chopped

1 cup cooked corn

8 cloves garlic

1 bunch cilantro

5 tablespoons peanut or vegetable oil

1 pound ground boar (or ground pork)

1 pound ground venison (or ground beef)

1 pound cubed venison (or cubed beef or pork steak)

15 ounces tomato puree

2 tablespoons chili powder

1 tablespoon cumin

1 tablespoon sumac

1 tablespoon paprika

1 teaspoon oregano

1 teaspoon marjoram

½ teaspoon cayenne

3 tablespoons tomato paste

6 ounces beer

1 quart beef broth

In a blender or food processor, combine onion, chiles, peppers, corn, garlic, and the stems from the cilantro and blend into a paste. This will be your sofrito. Set aside.

Add 2 tablespoons of oil to your stockpot and heat to high. Working in small batches, add your meat to the pot and brown for 1 to 2 minutes, just looking for color, not doneness. Set meat aside, juices and all.

Turn the heat down to medium and add 3 tablespoons of oil and the sofrito. Cook, stirring constantly, until the sofrito darkens to a beige-brown color, not burnt, and becomes fragrant. Stir in tomato paste and cook for another 2 minutes before adding the tomato puree and dried spices, cooking for another minute. Add beer, broth, and meat to the pot. Bring to a boil, then reduce to medium-low and simmer uncovered for 2 hours.

Remove from heat and serve with your favorite toppings. Chopped cilantro leaves, chives, sour cream, and cheese are always a winning combo.

CHILI CHEESE FRIES

The Winchesters had plenty of gripes about Chuck, but even they could admit he did create a few perfect things in this world. The '67 Impala. The sound of electric guitar wailing over pounding drums. And chili cheese fries. Sure, you can order these up in half the dive bars or greasy spoons anywhere in America. But there's nothing worse than getting your hopes up, only to have some mediocre line cook promise a work of art but deliver a heap of soggy trash. If you want something done right, you've got to do it yourself.

And it all starts with cooking up crisp and golden fries. You take the time to treat them right, they'll treat you to paradise. Now that you're already an expert in Bobby's three-meat savory and spicy chili, you've got the perfect carnivore's reward to smother those heavenly potatoes. Top it off to your own tastes, and bask in the finest glory of all creation.

---

2 large russet potatoes (about 2 pounds)
6 cups peanut oil (or other neutral oil with high smoke point)
1 cup Bobby's Hunter Chili (page 129)
1 cup Queso to Die For (page 123)
1 tablespoon chives or cilantro, for garnish

You're looking for ⅜-inch to ½-inch french fries, so start peeling. Or don't peel. Your potatoes—your preference. Cut the potatoes into slices ⅜ to ½ inches thick, then cut those into ⅜-to-½-inch planks. Soak for a few minutes and rinse fries twice in cold water to remove excess starch. Transfer to a clean bowl of water and refrigerate up to 8 hours or overnight. Drain and let potatoes dry out by laying them on a toweled sheet pan.

Working in small batches to be sure you don't overcrowd the fries or lower the temperature, blanch the fries in 300°F (150°C) oil for 5 minutes and set aside on a wire rack on top of a sheet pan, or paper towels, and let cool. Crank the heat up to 415°F (213°C) and, again working in batches, return the fries to the oil and fry until crisp and golden, about 2 to 5 minutes. Using a spider strainer, strain off oil and place the fries in a steel mixing bowl. Salt the fries to taste. Transfer fries to a plate, ladle on a layer of chili, and top with a layer of queso, or grated cheese of choice. Garnish with minced cilantro or chives.

Top the chili with Queso to Die For (page 123) to feel like you've died and gone to Heaven.

NICE PICKLE CHIPS

A bit less effective as a bargaining chip with Death (though he did admit to enjoying them), these addictive bits of fried and seasoned crunchy goodness still pack a killer amount of taste in every bite. Whether you need a zesty and lightly spiced crunchy companion keeping you sharp on the long drive to your next hunt, or just a more kick-ass snack for game day, these little bad boys are fried up to keep you fired up.

If you're getting enough fire dealing with demons all day, dip your chips into some cool and creamy herbed fresh ranch.

BASIL RANCH DIP:

- 2 tablespoons minced shallot
- 2 tablespoons chopped basil
- 2 tablespoons chopped chives
- 1 tablespoon dill
- 1 to 2 small cloves garlic, minced
- 2 teaspoons white wine vinegar
- ¾ cup mayonnaise
- 3 tablespoons sour cream
- 1 cup well-shaken buttermilk
- 1 pinch salt and freshly ground black pepper
- ¼ teaspoon smoked paprika (optional)

PICKLES:

- 1½ cup buttermilk
- 1 cup flour
- ½ teaspoon black pepper
- 1 teaspoon garlic powder
- ¼ teaspoon ground red pepper
- 2 tablespoons Cajun seasoning
- 1 tablespoon hot sauce
- 1 16-ounce jar dill pickle chips (or whole cut into ¼-inch rounds)
- 1 quart of peanut or vegetable oil for frying (you want about an inch of oil in your pan}
- 1 tablespoon finely chopped parsley
- ¼ cup beer (optional)

To make the dip, stir all ingredients together for a slightly chunky result, or use a blender for a finer dressing. Set aside.

To make the pickles, whisk together buttermilk, flour, spices, and hot sauce (add beer for a crispier, less dense batter) in a medium bowl.

Drain and dry pickle chips; this is important. Give them a squeeze and wrap in a towel to remove as much moisture as possible.

Using a deep skillet or saucepan, heat oil to 375°F and, working in batches, batter your pickle chips and carefully add to the oil. Flip until golden on both sides, about 2 to 4 minutes, and transfer to a wire rack to cool. Garnish with fresh chopped parsley and serve with basil ranch dip.

DEPARTMENT of INVESTIGATION
FBI
AGENT

BACON BURGER TURBO

Why do we do our work? Busting our butts every day, maybe all night, for pretty much no pay and even less recognition. Why suffer the licks and horrors of the job just to keep one little bit of the world running smoother? Dean Winchester sometimes said he did it so there was a tomorrow—and he could get another burger. You might chuckle it off, but he wasn't talking about fast food. When Dean dug down for that last bit of strength or grit or fight to muscle his way out of the jaws of death and save the day—or save the world!—THIS is the type of burger he was fighting for.

Juicy, sizzling marbled beef perfectly fried. Buttered and browned warm, hearty bun. Salty, sweet, and spicy maple bacon. Thickly poured rich and creamy queso. A totally indulgent caramelized onion garlic aioli. And a bit of sharp, crisp tang from some pickles. It might not be possible to taste all the things that make life worth living in one bite. But chase this with some good booze, and that should do it.

DEAN'S SECRET SAUCE:

1 clove of garlic, roasted

⅓ cup peanut or canola oil (or bacon fat)

⅔ cup extra-virgin olive oil

½ medium-large onion, caramelized (in bacon fat, preferably)

2 large egg yolks

4 teaspoons pickle juice

1 tablespoon fresh lemon juice

1 teaspoon yellow mustard

½ teaspoon salt (kosher or sea)

BURGER:

1 tablespoon butter

1 seeded burger bun

8 ounces ground beef (80/20 for best results)

2 slices Spicy Maple-Glazed Bacon (page 127)

Dean's Secret Sauce

Queso to Die For (page 123)

Pickles

For extra kick and crunch, use Nice Pickle Chips (page 131) instead.

To make Dean's secret sauce start by placing a bulb of garlic, with ¼ inches cut off the top and most of the papery exterior removed keeping the bulb intact, onto a sheet of aluminum foil. Drizzle 1 to 2 teaspoons of olive oil over the top and seal the foil into pouch and place into a 400°F (204°C) oven for 40 minutes or until brown and softened. Separately sauté your chopped onion in 1 teaspoon of olive oil over medium low heat until soft, brown, and caramelized—not burnt—about 20 minutes. Place your garlic and onion aside and begin to build your sauce by stirring together oils in a mixing cup. Put roasted garlic, lemon juice, caramelized onions, egg yolks, salt and pickle juice into a blender and pulse until a paste is formed. Turn the blender on medium speed and add oil to the mixture in a slow, thin stream until you've incorporated it all. The mixture should be the consistency of a thick mayonnaise. Fold in the mustard, place sauce into a sealed container, and store in the refrigerator until ready to use.

Heat a skillet over medium-high heat. Butter both halves of your bun and toast, flat side down. Remove buns from heat and set aside. Form and season your burger patty with salt and pepper on both sides and place on the hot skillet, no oil needed. Cook for about 4 minutes and flip, cooking for another 4 minutes.

Spoon a healthy amount of Dean's Secret Sauce on both top and bottom buns. Cut your bacon in half and place it on the bottom bun, followed by your patty. Spoon on your heated queso so that it coats the patty. Add pickles and top with the other half of the bun. Demolish and enjoy.

DINER
THE CLASSIC
GRILLED CHEESE
WITH CRISPY FRIES

Johnny Mac's

Water

THAT APPLE PIE

An apple pie can represent a lot. America. A warm and welcoming home. Some wholesome, sweet reward. Sam and Dean Winchester were known to use it as shorthand for the kind of life they'd likely never have as hunters—a life of peace and stability, with families of their own. That "apple pie life."

Ultimately, Sam Winchester found his own family, happiness, and old age that he'd almost given up on. While his brother Dean didn't—going down swinging against a nest of vampires—those who knew him can't help but feel Dean made that choice ages ago. And maybe his notorious love of pie itself was the consolation he took, savoring and treating himself to fleeting but joyous tastes of the sweet life he'd never commit to.

While Dean may have not been an avid baker, it's safe to assume he would appreciate this pie's layered tart-sweet baked apple flavor, the homey aroma and lingering spice of cinnamon, its flaky and buttery crusts—not to mention all that a perfectly warm and balanced pie represented. So, treat yourself to a slice of That Apple Pie. Add some cinnamon-rum ice cream to truly remind yourself how sweet life can be.

CINNAMON-RUM ICE CREAM:

2 cups heavy cream
1 cup whole milk
1 teaspoon grated cinnamon
6 egg yolks
¾ cup packed dark brown sugar
¼ cup Hot Mrs. Butters Rum (page 55)
1 teaspoon vanilla extract

9-inch unbaked pie crust (store-bought dough is fine, or use your favorite recipe)

PIE FILLING:

½ cup sour cream
1 cup sugar
3 tablespoons flour
1½ teaspoons vanilla extract
3 cups diced tart apple
2 eggs

PIE TOPPING:

¾ cups granulated sugar
½ cup flour
6 tablespoons softened butter
2 teaspoons ground cinnamon

Start with the ice cream. In a medium saucepan, bring the cream, milk, and cinnamon to a simmer over medium heat.

Meanwhile, in a mixing bowl, whisk together egg yolks and sugar until combined. Take your cream mixture off the heat and slowly whisk a steady stream into your egg mixture to temper. Once everything is combined in the bowl, transfer back to the saucepan over medium-low heat and stir until a thermometer reads 175°F (80°C) internally and the custard coats the back of a spoon.

Pull the custard from the heat and strain, using a fine mesh sieve, into a clean bowl. Stir in Hot Mrs. Butters Rum, cover, and place in the refrigerator for 4 to 6 hours to cool.

Once cooled, transfer the custard to your ice cream maker, adding the vanilla at this point while following the ice cream maker's instructions. Once complete, transfer your ice cream into a covered pint container and place in the freezer for 2 hours or until ready to enjoy.

To bake the pie shell, place your pie dough into a pie pan, line the pie dough with two layers of aluminum foil, and fill the foil-lined crust with pie weights. Parbake in the oven at 375°F (190°C) for 20 to 30 minutes. Remove crust from the oven, set aside, and reduce the oven heat to 300°F (150°C).

Meanwhile, in a blender or food processor, blend the sour cream, 1 cup sugar, 2 tablespoons flour, and 1½ tablespoons vanilla extract until combined. In a separate bowl, add diced apples and eggs and fold in the blended mixture. Remove foil from pie crust, add the filling, and place on the middle rack of the oven. Bake for 25 minutes. Remove and reduce oven heat to 250°F (120°C).

For the topping, whisk ¾ cup granulated sugar, ½ cup flour, 6 tablespoons softened butter, and 2 tablespoons cinnamon. Once combined, it should be a fine crumb consistency. Evenly coat the top of the pie with the mixture and place it back on the middle rack of the oven for 20 minutes. Let your pie cool for 1 to 4 hours. Serve with a scoop or two of cinnamon-rum ice cream.

BEER GUIDE

Truth is, when most hunters need a drink—Sam and Dean Winchester included—they'll usually just grab a beer. It's as plain and effective as the boys themselves. And the right beer can be as cool and calming as any hunter could hope to be in a crisis.

But for the uninitiated, the wide range of names and types of beers can be as inscrutable as trying to read the Angel Tablet. Every kind shares the same four ingredients—water, malt, hops, and yeast. Generally speaking, brews with heavier malt are sweeter, while those that push their hops tip the balance toward the bitter.

Of course, like the battle between good and evil, there's a million different kinds in between. And by changing the malts, hops, and yeast varieties, or introducing fruits and spices, we get an endless selection of styles and flavors. Hopefully, this shorthand guide can help rookies get started. Because there's always a perfect beer for any hunter, hunt, or victory celebration.

HOP FORWARD

American IPAs and Double IPAs (or go more generic with India pale ales)

Flavors: Light honey and caramel malt flavors that support a prominent hop bouquet of citrus, pine, stone, and tropical fruit notes

Aroma: A hop dominant range of floral, citrus, pine and fruit aromas over a subtle malt presence with hints of honey and light caramel

Body: Medium-low to full

Bitterness: Medium to very high

Suggested food pairing: The sharp and refreshing hop-forward flavors of a good IPA pair perfectly with something big, bad, and hearty like a monster sized serving of Chili Cheese Fries (page 131)

A favorite of: Sam Winchester

BLONDES AND PALE ALES

Flavors: Light to medium malt and honey flavors; in American pales, hops are more prominent with flavors of citrus and pine

Aroma: Cooked-cereal malt sweetness with slight to prominent hop presence

Body: Light to medium

Bitterness: Low to medium-high

Suggested food pairing: Light, refreshing, and palate pleasing, the perfect pub ale paired with the perfect pub snack: Nice Pickle Chips with basil ranch dip (page 131)

A favorite of: Garth Fitzgerald (special shout-out to Thighslapper Ale)

PILSNERS AND LIGHT LAGERS

Flavors: Crisp, clean, biscuit-like maltiness with an herbal and peppery hoppiness

Aroma: Clean pilsner malt notes of honey and lightly toasted bread with a sharp but delicate herbal hop aroma

Body: Low to medium

Bitterness: Low to high

Suggested food pairing: Opposites attract, and a light and crisp pilsner is a great contrast to the deep and cheesy broth of John Winchester's Kitchen Sink Stew (page 125).

A favorite of: Mary Winchester

MALT-CENTRIC

Reds and Ambers

Flavors: European varieties lean heavily on the caramel candy-like flavors from the malts and highlight their toasted maltiness, while American reds and ambers tend to up the hop flavors to a more prominent spot

Aroma: Rich malt aromas of chocolate, caramel and nuts with low to high degrees of hop presence

Body: Medium to full

Bitterness: Not present to high

Suggested food pairing: A good anytime beer needs a good anytime food pairing. Pig in a Poke with a side of maple mustard sauce (page 121) mixes sweet and savory in a most complementary combination

A favorite of: Charlie Bradbury

WHEAT ALES/HEFEWEIZENS AND WITBIERS

Flavors: Yeast supplies the bulk of the flavors here, with phenolic notes of cloves, nutmeg, and vanilla, as well as stray tones of ripe banana. In witbiers, the use of a spice mixture paired with sweet-and-sour orange peels is prevalent

Aroma: Bananas and bubblegum; Orange and coriander

Body: Light to full

Bitterness: Not present to low

Suggested Pairing: A great companion to Sam's Health Quake Shake (page 126), with all those oh-so-good-for-you vitamin-rich nutrients found in this hazy, yeast-filled beer

A favorite of: Bobby Singer (but damned if he's going to try to pronounce it all German-like)

BROWNS AND PORTERS

Flavors: Light to dark caramel, sweet malt, and chocolate

Aroma: Sweet and roasted malts, caramel candy, and chocolate.

Body: Medium to full

Bitterness: Very low to medium

Suggested food pairing: A rich and hearty brown, or porter, and John Winchester's Kitchen Sink Stew (page 125) makes for a happy hunter.

A favorite of: Kevin Tran, Meg

STOUTS

Flavors: Roasted dark malts with coffee, caramel, and rich chocolate notes

Aromas: Roasted malt, coffee, caramel, and chocolate

Body: Medium-light to full

Bitterness: Low to very high

Suggested food pairing: Excellent choice to complement the spicy, hearty richness of Bobby's Hunter Chili (page 129)

A favorite of: Dean Winchester, John Winchester

WILD ALES AND SOURS

Flavors: Light, tart fruit and sour candies; some lean more toward rich and malty, with deep vinegar notes

Aroma: Stone fruits, berries, bright sour notes, red wine, and balsamic vinegar aromas are prevalent.

Body: Dry to full

Bitterness: Very low

Suggested food pairing: These wild and exciting beers are so rich in flavor and nuance that the only suitable food pairing is an equally flavorful and nuanced . . . cheeseburger! Uncommon but a thick and juicy Bacon Burger Turbo (page 133) with a semi tart German berliner weisse or a spicy wild belgian saison is a match made in Winchester heaven

A favorite of: Werewolves, Crowley

MEAD

Flavors: Rich honey sweetness with notes of peaches, lemon, and marmalade

Aroma: Citrus, apple, and floral aromas prevail

Body: Low to medium

Bitterness: Not present to very low

Suggested food pairing: Some drinks pair perfectly with food and other demand a spirit on the side. Which is why Hot Apple (page 85) is the perfect complement to this deeply rich and sweet nectar of the ancients

A favorite of: Chuck Shurley, but "they stopped making the really good stuff in 3,000 BCE."

CIDER

Flavors: While American and English varieties tend to lean on the sweet juice-like flavor of sweet apples, older interpretations from the Basque regions of Spain and France embrace the entire spectrum of the apple from tart to sweet. The open wild fermentation adds a slightly sour and refreshing nuance

Aroma: Sweet and tart apples, citrusy and floral

Body: Light and crisp to medium

Bitterness: Not present to slightly tart (though some modern cider houses have introduced hops)

Suggested food pairing: That Apple Pie (page 137)! The sweet and sometimes tart flavors of a cider are harmoniously paired with a sour cream apple pie and a scoop of cinnamon-rum ice cream

A favorite of: Lucifer, Eve

ABOUT THE AUTHORS

Adam Carbonell is a San Diego–based mixologist and educator with over 20 years' experience in the food and beverage industry, specifically the prestigious San Diego craft beer scene. As a professional brewer he strove to innovate the beer space by bridging the gap between kitchen and brewery with a reputation for working directly with local farmers, sourcing and processing fresh ingredients by hand. During his years of working with some of the world's most prestigious breweries and overseeing every aspect of the brewing process, from production to distribution and marketing, he transitioned to the nonprofit sector, taking the role of San Diego Brewers Guild President helping to promote and grow the San Diego craft beer market, co-founding San Diego Beer Week in the process.

After years working as a brewery contractor and consultant he gradually found his way to the front of the house in the infancy of San Diego's cocktail boom, and he's still there. Adam enjoys getting to connect daily with guests on a personal level over handcrafted libations, but also as an educator and lecturer he gets to spread the good word of distilled spirits and cocktails to a worldwide audience.

James Asmus is a writer of books, theater, comedy, video games, and TV. His published work includes over a dozen Marvel Comics titles including Gambit, Captain America, and Amazing Spider-Man, Rick & Morty, the Transformers / My Little Pony crossover for IDW, and a reimagining of QUANTUM and WOODY for Valiant (which snagged five Harvey Award nominations, including Best Writer). James has also written original series like the Manning Award–nominated apocalyptic buddy comedy End Times of Bram & Ben, action satire Survival Street, all-ages sci-fi dark comedy Field Tripping, plus body horror series Evolution and Thief Of Thieves for Skybound (with Walking Dead creator Robert Kirkman). In TV, he's written for Marvel Hero Project and Marvel Video Comics as well as written and produced shows for History and Discovery networks. James lives outside Portland, OR, with his wife and two weirdly wonderful kids.

INSIGHT
EDITIONS

PO Box 3088
San Rafael, CA 94912
www.insighteditions.com

Find us on Facebook: www.facebook.com/InsightEditions
Follow us on Instagram: @insightedition

ISBN: 979-8-88663-090-9

Publisher: Raoul Goff
VP, Co-Publisher: Vanessa Lopez
VP, Creative: Chrissy Kwasnik
VP, Manufacturing: Alix Nicholaeff
VP, Group Managing Editor: Vicki Jaeger
Publishing Director: Jamie Thompson
Designer: Brooke McCullum
Executive Editor: Jennifer Sims
Editorial Assistants: Jennifer Pellman, Sadie Lowry
Managing Editor: Maria Spano
Senior Production Editor: Michael Hylton
Production Associate: Deena Hashem
Senior Production Manager, Subsidiary Rights: Lina s Palma-Temena
Photography by Waterbury Publications, Inc

ROOTS of PEACE REPLANTED PAPER

Insight Editions, in association with Roots of Peace, will plant two trees for each tree used in the manufacturing of this book. Roots of Peace is an internationally renowned humanitarian organization dedicated to eradicating land mines worldwide and converting war-torn lands into productive farms and wildlife habitats. Roots of Peace will plant two million fruit and nut trees in Afghanistan and provide farmers there with the skills and support necessary for sustainable land use.

Manufactured in China by Insight Editions

10 9 8 7 6 5 4 3